Creating Business Applications with Office 365

Techniques in SharePoint, PowerApps, Power BI, and More

Jeffrey M. Rhodes

Creating Business Applications with Office 365: Techniques in SharePoint, PowerApps, Power BI, and More

Jeffrey M. Rhodes
Colorado, CO, USA

ISBN-13 (pbk): 978-1-4842-5330-4   ISBN-13 (electronic): 978-1-4842-5331-1
https://doi.org/10.1007/978-1-4842-5331-1

Copyright © 2019 by Jeffrey M. Rhodes

Managing Director, Apress Media LLC: Welmoed Spahr
Acquisitions Editor: Smriti Srivastava
Development Editor: Laura Berendson
Coordinating Editor: Shrikant Vishwakarma

Cover designed by eStudioCalamar

Cover image designed by Freepik (www.freepik.com)

Distributed to the book trade worldwide by Springer Science+Business Media New York, 233 Spring Street, 6th Floor, New York, NY 10013. Phone 1-800-SPRINGER, fax (201) 348-4505, e-mail orders-ny@springer-sbm.com, or visit www.springeronline.com. Apress Media, LLC is a California LLC and the sole member (owner) is Springer Science + Business Media Finance Inc (SSBM Finance Inc). SSBM Finance Inc is a **Delaware** corporation.

For information on translations, please e-mail rights@apress.com, or visit http://www.apress. com/rights-permissions.

Apress titles may be purchased in bulk for academic, corporate, or promotional use. eBook versions and licenses are also available for most titles. For more information, reference our Print and eBook Bulk Sales web page at http://www.apress.com/bulk-sales.

Any source code or other supplementary material referenced by the author in this book is available to readers on GitHub via the book's product page, located at www.apress.com/978-1-4842-5330-4. For more detailed information, please visit http://www.apress.com/source-code.

Printed on acid-free paper

This book is dedicated to my friend and mentor, Brigadier General Erlind G. "Lindy" Royer, USAF, Retired.

Dedication

Quite a bit has changed since my last book, 2009's *Programming for e-Learning Developers*. Although I greatly enjoyed my 19 years of running a software company, I decided to return to my alma mater, the U.S. Air Force Academy (USAFA), first as a Senior IT Specialist and more recently as the Academic Chief Technical Officer. My sincere appreciation goes to my bosses in both the 10th Communications Squadron and in the Dean of Faculty for taking a chance on someone who had never used SharePoint or worked at a college (other than as an adjunct Economics teacher): Mr. Joe McKeehan, Mr. Neland North, Colonel Tom Swoveland, Colonel Joyce Storm, and Colonel Doug Mellars. What sealed the deal for both of these positions – as with other opportunities in my life – was a strong recommendation by my mentor (and the former Dean of Faculty at USAFA), Brigadier General Royer, PhD.

I first met Lindy[1] in the Fall of 1984 when I was a sophomore at USAFA and he was the Head of the Electrical Engineering Department. He happened to be my instructor in the core circuits course. After a couple of exams, he wrote a note on my paper asking if I had considered Electrical Engineering as a major. Although I had already declared Astronautical Engineering as a major, I went to see him. Lindy asked what my goals were and, finding out that I wanted to be a Rhodes scholar, called up his friend and colleague, Colonel Malham Wakin.[2] Colonel Wakin connected me with Ms. Fern Kinion in the Scholarship Office, eventually leading

---

[1] Of course I exclusively called him Colonel Royer then ☺.

[2] Colonel Wakin (now Brigadier General, USAF, Retired) is a lion in military ethics and morality of war. He was the long-time Head of the Philosophy Department at USAFA. His books on Amazon can be found at https://tinyurl.com/y7chumnk.

to my becoming the first cadet to win a British Marshall Scholarship while at USAFA. Lindy became my advisor and mentor. His letter of recommendation was a key factor in winning that scholarship. At least once a week, my future wife Sue and I would stop by his office to say hi on the way to dinner (he pretty much always worked late ☺).

The picture in Figure 1 is from graduation after I received a medal from the country of Chile that goes to the #1 graduate in each class. Around the same time, Lindy was selected as USAFA Dean of Faculty and promoted to Brigadier General.

Fast-forward 5 years and I had decided to leave the Air Force.[3] Although Lindy recommended that I stay in the Air Force, he gave me a job in the new commercial business he was building as part of Titan Corporation. It was there that I discovered an affinity for writing software, particularly in the e-learning field. Four years later, the hardest part of starting my own company, Platte Canyon Multimedia Software Corporation, was telling Lindy that I was leaving. He was fully supportive and even jumped in to help when I needed sage advice over the years.

Figure 1. Colonel Lindy Royer and Cadet Jeff Rhodes – 1987

---

[3]At the time I thought I wanted to get into politics. I was also undecided if I wanted to make the Air Force a career. The incentive was either to stay at least 20 years (when you are eligible for retirement) or get out as soon as you are eligible. I didn't understand how valuable that retirement was; I'm lucky that I have been able to buy those years back now that I have joined Civil Service.

When I decided to return to the Air Force as a Federal civilian in 2015, Lindy was very supportive and closed the deal by serving as a reference as I mentioned. He continues to serve as Vice President of the *Friends of the Air Force Academy Library* among other endeavors. Figure 2 shows a more recent picture of us. Lindy is an inspiration to me and many others!

Figure 2. *Lindy Royer and me next to my USAFA office – 2018*

Table of Contents

About the Author

**Jeffrey M. Rhodes** is the Academic Chief Technical Officer at the United States Air Force Academy. Prior to that, he was a Senior IT Specialist in charge of SharePoint, Remedy, and other key systems at the Academy. Jeff was the founder and Chief Technical Officer of Platte Canyon Multimedia Software Corporation, a leader in developing commercial e-learning software. He graduated at the top of his class at the Air Force Academy, where he earned a Bachelor of Science in Electrical Engineering. Jeff received a master's degree in Economics from the London School of Economics, which he attended under a British Marshall Scholarship. He is the author of *Programming for e-Learning Developers: ToolBook, Flash, JavaScript, and Silverlight*; *VBTrain.Net: Creating Computer and Web Based Training with Visual Basic .NET*; and *The ToolBook Companion*. He lives in Colorado Springs with his wife Sue and is the proud father of his sons Derek and Michael.

About the Technical Reviewers

Arun Sharma is leading the Cloud business at Paytm Cloud across the regions as General Manager, Enterprise Cloud. He has vast experience on cloud technologies (Microsoft Azure, AWS, G Suite), IoT, ML, Microservices, Bots, Docker, and Containerization. He has almost 17 years of experience in a wide variety of roles such as Delivery Manager at Microsoft, Product Manager at Icertis, Lead and Architect Associate at Infosys, Executive Trainer at Aptech, and Development Consultant at CMC. He managed relationship, sales, cloud consumption, consulting services, and adoption with medium- and large-size global customers.

Arun loves challenges in the Microsoft playing field combining it with his domain knowledge in banking, insurance, FMCG, government (local), retail, and telecom. He is very active in community as author of international research papers, technical speaker, reviewer, blogger, and LinkedIn Sales Navigator. He is also recognized with the title of MCT from Microsoft and pursuing Doctor of Business Administration post his M.B.A. and M.Tech. (CS). Arun Sharma can be found on Twitter at **@arunkhoj**.

Devendra G. Asane is working as a Cloud, Big Data, and Microservices Architect with Persistent Systems. Prior to this, he has worked with Microsoft.

Devendra lives with his wife Seema and son Teerthank in Pune, India.

See his complete profile on www.linkedin.com/in/devendra007.

Acknowledgments

Massive thanks go to my wife Sue. You are always loving and supportive. Asking you to marry me 31+ years ago was the best decision of my life.

From the time of my first book (2001), my sons Derek and Michael went from being in their first decade of life to college graduates and exceptional members of society. I am proud of your accomplishments and even prouder of the men you have become.

Finally, I would like to thank my sister Joni and my brother Jim. We've been very close our whole lives, and it has been a tremendous blessing. Joni is the rock of our family and the host of every family event. You will not find anyone with a bigger heart. Jim has endured tremendous physical struggles but perseveres with an amazingly positive attitude. Thanks for always loving and taking care of your little brother!

Introduction

This book is targeted at power users and what I call business developers. While some of the applications and techniques require a degree of understanding programming, my objective is to make the solutions accessible to the non-computer scientist.[1] We are looking at client-side solutions that can be accomplished with the built-in Office 365 applications (primarily SharePoint, PowerApps, Flow, Forms, and Power BI) as well as additional SharePoint capabilities using JavaScript, InfoPath, and/or SharePoint Designer. The solutions target Office 365[2] except where noted, but many of the SharePoint solutions will work in SharePoint 2013 or older versions as well.

Audience Level

While some programming expertise will be helpful for some of the more advanced examples, we do *not* assume that you are a programmer. Anyone who is willing to learn and feels at home in front of a keyboard is welcome.

---

[1]Which I am as well. My undergraduate degree is in Electrical Engineering, while my master's is in Economics.

[2]Most examples are for the version of SharePoint included with Office 365 for Business Plan. Some features shown, particularly *Microsoft Forms* and publishing to *Power BI*, use Office 365 for Education.

A Bit of Background

What makes me qualified to write a book like this? I mentioned in the "Acknowledgments" section that I had never used SharePoint until I started at the Air Force Academy in March 2015. At that time, we were migrating from SharePoint 2010 to 2013. I found that my skills in JavaScript, jQuery, Cascading Style Sheets (CSS), REpresentational State Transfer (REST), and general programming served me well and gave me the baseline to explore SharePoint's capabilities, particularly adding JavaScript/jQuery and taking advantage of InfoPath and SharePoint Designer.

Separately at first, I discovered *Power BI* and started using it to visualize SharePoint surveys, Excel spreadsheets, Remedy tickets,[3] and Access databases. When we moved to Office 365 at the Academy, we now had Power BI in the browser as well as *PowerApps*, *Flow*, and *Forms* to add more power. I particularly fell in love with PowerApps, as you will see in the chapters to come.

I hope you can apply some or all of these solutions in your environment.

---

[3]I managed our BMC Remedy help ticketing environment. I found that pointing Power BI directly at the SQL Server database allowed for much improved ticket tracking and displaying survey results. We cover that solution later in this book.

CHAPTER 1

Enabling SharePoint Designer and Custom Scripting

Many of the SharePoint solutions to follow involve either connecting with *SharePoint Designer* or injecting custom JavaScript, Hypertext Markup Language (HTML), and/or Cascading Style Sheets (CSS) content into a SharePoint page. Both of these are disabled by default in Office 365. Fortunately, the same solution described in the following fixes both issues.

For injecting JavaScript, HTML, and/or CSS, I typically insert a *Content Editor* web part. However, Office 365 "modern" pages are missing both the *Content Editor* and *Script Editor* as shown in Figure 3.

Figure 3. *Missing Content Editor in Office 365*

© Jeffrey M. Rhodes 2019
J. M. Rhodes, *Creating Business Applications with Office 365*,
https://doi.org/10.1007/978-1-4842-5331-1_1

If you have administrator rights, you can follow the steps listed next to add the *Content Editor* back. If not, you can pass this along to an administrator. If you are using an older version of SharePoint, the *Content Editor* will already be there.

Figure 4. *Office 365 dashboard showing the Admin button*

1. Go to the Office 365 dashboard and select *Admin* as shown in Figure 4.

2. Select the SharePoint *admin center*.

3. Select *settings*.

4. Finally, choose the options *Allow users to run custom script on personal sites* as well as *Allow users to run custom script on self-service created sites*. Notice the warning that changes might take up to 24 hours. All of these options are shown in Figure 5.

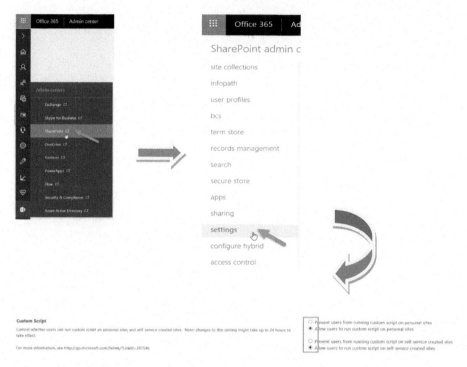

Figure 5. *Opening the SharePoint admin center and allowing users to run custom scripts*

Once Office 365 has updated the settings, Figure 6 shows that the *Content Editor* is now available.

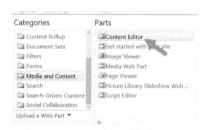

Figure 6. *Content Editor available after updating SharePoint settings*

CHAPTER 2

Updating a SharePoint List Using PowerApps

PowerApps[1] is a powerful new form tool in Office 365. It is not a direct replacement of *InfoPath* (which we also use in this book) as it does things differently (and often better). I particularly like that PowerApps can be created completely in the browser, are optimized for mobile devices, can connect to a multitude of data sources, and have a familiar Visual Basic-like syntax.[2]

In this chapter, we will build a simple application to view and update a SharePoint list. Our overall objective is to create a help ticketing system with these requirements:

- Users will fill out a form when they arrive in person at the help desk. It will only include information that they know such as issue, description, who they are, and their department.

---

[1] I found Shane Young of BoldZebras' YouTube channel helpful for learning about PowerApps: www.youtube.com/channel/UC7_OGRP8BYvtGB8eZdPG6Ng.

[2] For example, by using the & to concatenate values. I'm a big Visual Basic fan and actually wrote a previous book called *VBTrain.Net: Creating Computer and Web Based Training with Visual Basic .NET*.

© Jeffrey M. Rhodes 2019
J. M. Rhodes, *Creating Business Applications with Office 365*,
https://doi.org/10.1007/978-1-4842-5331-1_2

- Technicians see new items by default but can search for existing items. They can set additional information such as the status, issue category, assigned technician, and notes. Technicians can also add items for situations like phone and email support.

We will build the data source (SharePoint list), make relatively minor changes to the default form, and then create another form to add to or update the list. We will then continue the development in Chapter 15.

Figure 7 shows our SharePoint list along with the default form. Notice that clicking the *Customize with PowerApps* link launches PowerApps.

Figure 7. *Help Tickets SharePoint list with corresponding SharePoint form. Clicking Customize with PowerApps launches PowerApps*

Customizing the form won't meet all our requirements only a single form can be launched when the user clicks *New* (we want separate forms for users and technicians). Plus, we don't want to have to go to the SharePoint site at all. We want to make all edits via PowerApps. The SharePoint site will instead mainly be a *Power BI* data source for visualizations showing our ticket information.[3]

There is still some value in customizing the form as it gives us nice new capabilities and helps us learn PowerApps. One of the first things you will notice in our customized form is that the *Description* is now only a single line. Figure 8 shows how we drag the *Height* to give more space and then set the *Mode* property to be *TextMode.MultiLine*. While we were at it, we set the *HintText* property to give the user more instructions on what to do.

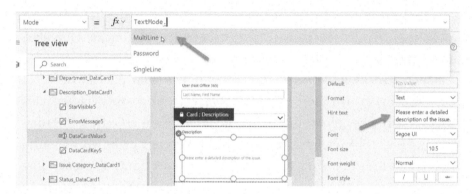

Figure 8. *Updating the Height, HintText, and Mode properties of the Description input*

Figure 9 shows the resulting form in SharePoint.

---

[3]We will dig deep into Power BI in later chapters. Another use of SharePoint would be to have a "New Tickets" view that could be sorted by date and time. Technicians could use to determine who has been waiting longest and call that person next. We hope to build this into the PowerApps technician application as well.

Figure 9. *New Item form customized with PowerApps*

More powerful in our case will be to use PowerApps to create a mobile-friendly application for adding, deleting, and editing items as well as searching. To do that, we launch PowerApps directly from our Office 365 home screen. We then choose the *Start from data* Canvas app. This default to the *phone* size (the other choice we can do from a blank app is *tablet*). From there, we select SharePoint as our data source. We enter in the URL for our site (just include the site and not the list). Figure 10 shows the result. Notice how PowerApps created the screens for browsing the data, viewing the details, and editing the data. We update the *App name* and *Description* properties and then set the application to *Confirm exit* and then set a corresponding message.

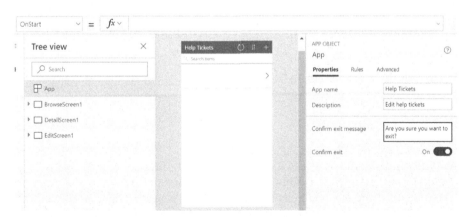

Figure 10. *PowerApps application with Browse, Details, and Edit screens*

8

We could do extensive edits as needed within PowerApps, but we will save this for a more customized solution in Chapter 15. For now, we will save[4] and then share it with other users. Figure 11 shows the resulting *New Item* screen. Notice that we could access this with the *PowerApps* mobile application as well.

Figure 11. *New Item screen for Help Tickets list*

---

[4]Be sure to save immediately as automatic saving does not kick in until you save the application the first time.

CHAPTER 3

Customizing Date Displays with jQuery

One of richest opportunities for customizing SharePoint functionality is by using JavaScript and, in particular, the popular open source library, *jQuery*.[1] At the Air Force Academy, we added it as well as the *jQuery UI*[2] set of controls to our master pages, making the libraries available on every page in our environment. I won't do that with these Office 365 examples, but it is fairly easy to link to them directly.

In this example, the customer asked for dates in a *Task List* to show up in amber when the *Due to Director* or *Overall Suspense* dates are within 7 days of the current date. The dates need to be in red once those dates have passed. As shown in Figure 12, the *Due to Director* already shows up in red since that functionality is built in for the *Due Date* column only. But we need jQuery to help us with the rest.

---

[1]Learn more, download, contribute, and read the documentation at `http://jquery.com`.

[2]jQuery UI allows you to "skin" controls with a standard or customized theme. I've used the *Button* and *Dialog* controls extensively in SharePoint and the rest of the controls in other applications. We cover this in the next chapter. Visit `http://jqueryui.com` to learn more.

© Jeffrey M. Rhodes 2019
J. M. Rhodes, *Creating Business Applications with Office 365*,
https://doi.org/10.1007/978-1-4842-5331-1_3

	Task #	Date Received	Task Name	Assigned To	% Complete	Due to Director	Overall Suspense		Task Status

March 2   March 8   March 13

Task 1
3/1 – 4/3

⊕ new task

All Tasks   Calendar   Completed   ···   Find an item 🔍

▲ Tasker Type : **Inbound** (1)

  ▲ Task Status : (1)

     2018-001   March 1   Task 1 ⊞   ···   50 %   April 3   4/20/2018

▲ Tasker Type : **Outbound** (2)

  ▲ Task Status : In Progress (2)

     2018-100   April 1   Task 2 ⊞   ···   50 %   May 3   5/25/2018   In Progress

     2018-101   March 11   Task 3 ⊞   ···   50 %   July 13   7/31/2018   In Progress

Figure 12. *Task List before customization*

The general approach will be to properly format the date display, look at the generated HTML, use jQuery to select that element,[3] and then modify it.

Format the Date Display

The first step is to eliminate the "friendly" date format that eliminates the year as well as uses description like "today" and "yesterday." Instead, we want the *Standard* format of mm/dd/yyyy. We do this by editing the column settings as shown in Figure 13. This will allow us to compare these dates in our JavaScript.

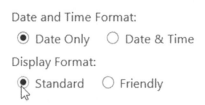

Date and Time Format:

  ◉ Date Only   ○ Date & Time

Display Format:

  ◉ Standard   ○ Friendly

Figure 13. *Standard Display Format for date columns for manipulation via JavaScript*

---

[3]This is the main reason to use jQuery rather than JavaScript on its own. jQuery makes it very easy to find elements by their attributes. For example, say you had this div: <div id="xyz"></div>. You could reference it programmatically via JavaScript like this: `var elementId = document.getElementById("xyz");`. With jQuery, it is easier with this syntax: `var elementId = $("#xyz");`.

Find the Information in the HTML

The next step is to use the Developer Tools in your browser to inspect the generated HTML in order to figure out a strategy for finding the dates that we want. Figure 14 shows the Developer Tools in Microsoft Edge. We use the *DOM*[4] *Explorer* and select one of the items we want. Microsoft didn't make it easy for us in this case, since the *span* doesn't have an *id* or a unique class. Moving up a level to the table cell (*td*) has more promise. It has a combination of classes (*ms-cellstyle* and *ms-vb2*). Plus, we need the 8th and 9th columns.[5]

Figure 14. *Developer Tools in Microsoft Edge showing the ms-cellstyle ms-vb2 class*

In words, we now have a plan. Find the dates in the 3rd, 8th, and 9th columns of any table on the page. Compare the date to the current date. For those within 7 days, change their color to amber. For those that are in the past, change them to red. We will define classes (CSS) for these colors.

---

[4]DOM stands for Document Object Model, which is basically all the HTML on the page.

[5]You need to use the Developer Tools to count them since one of the columns does not show up on the screen and the other one holds the menu (...). Note that we start counting at 1 in this case (unlike many programming contexts where we start from 0).

Add Styles and JavaScript to a Text File

Our technique is to add our styles and programming to a text file, upload that to a document library, and then point a *Content Editor* web part to that file. This is much easier to maintain than putting the code directly into a *Script Editor* web part, and it also allows us to use the same file on multiple pages. Listing 1 shows the contents of the text file.

Listing 1. Styles and JavaScript for updating date displays for task lists

```
<style>
    .alert {
        color: #b79a16;
        font-weight: bold;
    }

    .overdue {
        color: #d72a18;
        font-weight: bold;
    }

    .ms-error {
        color: #d72a18 !important;
        font-weight: bold !important;
    }
 </style>

<script src="https://code.jquery.com/jquery-3.3.1.min.js">
</script>

<script>

    var today = new Date();
    var numDaysToShowAlert = 7;
    var existingProcessImn = ProcessImn;
```

```
// need to operate on both date due to director and overall
   suspense
$(function () {
    FindTableElements();
});

ProcessImn = function () {
    var results = existingProcessImn.apply(this, arguments);

    FindTableElements();
    return results;
}

function FindTableElements() {
    $("table tr td:nth-child(8)").each(function () {
        var cellId = $(this);

        UpdateDateDisplay(cellId);
    });

    $("table tr td:nth-child(9)").each(function () {
        var cellId = $(this);

        UpdateDateDisplay(cellId);
    });
}

function UpdateDateDisplay(cellId) {
    var dateText = cellId.text();

    if (dateText != "") {
        var dateVal = new Date(dateText);
        var numDays = DateDiff(dateVal, today);
```

```
            if (numDays < -1) { // use -1 since date starts at
                                   midnight and items due that
                                   day show overdue if use 0
                cellId.addClass("overdue");
            }
            else {
                if (numDays <= numDaysToShowAlert) {
                    cellId.addClass("alert");
                }
            }
        }
    }

    function DateDiff(date1, date2) {
        var datediff = date1.getTime() - date2.getTime();
        //store the getTime diff - or +
        return (datediff / (24 * 60 * 60 * 1000));
        //Convert values to -/+ days and return value
    }
```

</script>

We first define an *alert* and an *overdue* class.[6] The colors are RGB (red, green, blue) in hexadecimal format. Again by digging into the generated HTML, we see that SharePoint itself uses its *ms-error* class for its built-in functionality to turn dates red. Since we don't want two different colors of red, we use the *!important* keyword to change that class and make our version dominant. The next line links to jQuery from a content delivery

---

[6]The . at the beginning of *.alert* means that this is a class. A # means that we match an id, while no punctuation such as *tr* means that the style applies to all elements of that type.

network (CDN).[7] If your site is not available on the Internet, you may want to locate jQuery on your own farm and link to it from there.

Getting to the JavaScript, we define a *today* variable and initialize it to the current date and time (via JavaScripts *new Date()*). To make our code flexible, we define *numDaysToShowAlert* as a variable. So if we wanted to change the functionality to go amber 10 days out, we could just change the variable value. This also makes the rest of our code more readable.

The next line comes from the fact that the view has grouping (first by *Tasker Type* and then by *Task Status*) as we saw back in Figure 12. SharePoint doesn't render the table until you click to expand the group. *ProcessImn* is the function that is called when this happens. We assign this to a variable (*existingProcessImn*) so that we can modify it later in the script.

The next part [*$(function() ...*] is jQuery shorthand for its *document. ready* function. It is important because jQuery makes sure not to call this function until the page is fully loaded into the browser.[8] If we are using a view that does not have grouping, this function would be sufficient for finding our dates. So we call our custom *FindTableElements* function, which we will explain in the following.

---

[7]Be sure to use an https:// link. My first version with an http:// link failed for security reasons.

[8]This is important since otherwise the JavaScript code might look for HTML elements that have not yet been loaded and thus are not available for interaction or changing.

Figure 15. *Setting the Content Link, Title, and Chrome State*

The next set of code redefines the *ProcessImn* function. We let it operate [*existingProcessImn.apply(…)*] and store its return value. Remember that this function gets called after our view is expanded. So we now call our *FindTableElements* function. We then return our *results* so that SharePoint can continue its operation.

Within *FindTableElements*, we see the power of jQuery. The key line is *$("table tr td:nth-child(8)").each(function () {*. This means to find all objects that are in a table, row (tr), and column (td). Find the 8th child (e.g., the 8th column). Then call the following function for each one. Within the function, we create a jQuery object with the *$(this)* syntax. We then call a *UpdateDateDisplay* function, passing this object as a parameter. We then do the same thing with the 9th child.

Within *UpdateDateDisplay,* we use the jQuery *text* function to read the text of the table column. If it is not blank, we create a *Date* object[9] from it. We then call a custom *DateDiff* function, which converts both dates (the value from the column as well as our *today* variable) to seconds, does the match to find the number of seconds between them, and then converts them back to days. If the date has already passed, we use the jQuery *addClass* method to set the cell's class to our *overdue* style. If not, we check to see if we are within *numDaysToShowAlert* and, if so, set the class to *alert*.

Add the Text File to Our SharePoint Page

Now that we understand the code, let's add it to page. We first upload the text file to a document library.[10]

Click the file and copy the location out of the address bar (`https://plattecanyon.sharepoint.com/samples/CodeLibrary/colorDatesBasedOnSuspense.txt` in our example). Add a *Content Editor* web part (see Figure 6). Edit *Web Part* properties as shown in Figure 15. We paste in the *Content Link* path. For the *Title*, I look to put in something like "JavaScript Code – Do Not Delete." We then set the *Chrome State* to *None* so that the title only shows up when a developer is editing the page.

Your code is NOT likely to work correctly the first time, so being able to debug it is critical. We again use the Developer Tools. Go to the *Debugger* tab (Edge or Internet Explorer) or *Sources* tab (Chrome). I find it easier to search for a known value in the code, such as *UpdateDateDisplay* in our example. Then set breakpoints as shown in Figure 16. Then refresh the page. From there, you can view variables, add more breakpoints, and so on. For example, Figure 17 shows the values of the local variables.

---

[9]Recall that we changed the column settings to show a standard display. This step would have failed if we had a column value of April 1 or Yesterday.

[10]I usually call it *Code Library* so that it doesn't get mixed up with other documents.

Figure 16. *Setting a breakpoint after searching for UpdateDateDisplay*

Figure 17. *Debugger showing values of dateText, dateVal, and numDays variables*

Once everything is working correctly, the results look like those in Figure 18.

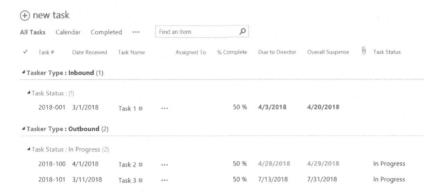

Figure 18. *Task List after customization*

CHAPTER 4

Adding jQuery UI Controls

I've used *jQuery UI* for many years (`http://jqueryui.com`) to easily create "skinnable" widgets such as buttons and dialog boxes. When we stood up our SharePoint 2013 environment at the Air Force Academy back in 2015, I created a custom theme matching our colors and put the references to it, the jQuery library itself, and jQuery UI all into the SharePoint master pages. With Office 365, we are getting away from master pages, but we can still take advantage of jQuery UI. Figure 19 shows our sample page. The buttons use the *Redmond* theme. When the user clicks a button, the corresponding site is shown in a popup window.

Figure 19. *jQuery UI Button sample page*

© Jeffrey M. Rhodes 2019
J. M. Rhodes, *Creating Business Applications with Office 365*,
https://doi.org/10.1007/978-1-4842-5331-1_4

21

As with the previous chapter, we put the styles, JavaScript, and HTML in a single text file, upload it to a document library, and then link to it from a *Content Editor*. Listing 2 shows the inline styles and links to external files.

Listing 2. Styles and script references for jQuery UI Button example

```
<style>
    #MainPageLinkButtons ul {
        list-style: none;
    }

        #MainPageLinkButtons ul li {
            display: inline-block;
            padding: 3px;
        }

    .O365Buttons {
        width: 150px;
    }
</style>

<script src="https://code.jquery.com/jquery-3.3.1.min.js"></
script>
<script src="https://code.jquery.com/ui/1.12.1/jquery-ui.js"></
script>
<link rel="stylesheet" type="text/css" href="https://code.
jquery.com/ui/1.12.1/themes/redmond/jquery-ui.css">
```

Our first two styles are a CSS trick to put the buttons inside the *unordered list* and *list item* combination to get dynamic spacing on the page. If you have more horizontal space available, then the buttons will move up to the same line. We turn off the normal display with *list-style: none,* get our *inline-block* layout, and add some *padding*. We make the buttons all the same width with the *O365Buttons* class. We then link to our

22

external *jQuery* and *jQuery UI* JavaScript files as well as the *Redmond* skin for the buttons via the *css* file. Listing 4 shows us the JavaScript.

Listing 3. JavaScript for jQuery UI Button example

```
<script type="text/javascript">
    $(function () {
        $("#Google").button().click(function () {
            showO365Window("https://www.google.com", "Google");

            return false;
        });

        $("#LinkedIn").button().click(function () {
            showO365Window("https://www.linkedin.com",
            "LinkedIn");

            return false;
        });

        $("#FaceBook").button().click(function () {
            showO365Window("https://www.facebook.com",
            "FaceBook");

            return false;
        });

        $("#Twitter").button().click(function () {
            showO365Window("https://www.twitter.com",
            "Twitter");

            return false;
        });

        $("#Bing").button().click(function () {
            showO365Window("https://www.bing.com", "Bing");
```

```
            return false;
        });

        $("#Microsoft").button().click(function () {
            showO365Window("http://www.usafasupport.com/home.
            html", "Microsoft");

            return false;
        });

    function showO365Window(url, windowName) {
        window.open(url, windowName, "width=800, height=600,
        left=0, top=0, resizable=yes, scrollbars=yes");

        return false; // so button doesn't post-back
    }
</script>
```

As we have seen previously, the *$(function() {});* means that this code
will run as soon as the page is fully loaded. In each case, we reference
the *id* of the HTML element using the # symbol. So *$("#Google")* returns
a reference to the HTML element with an id of Google. See Listing 4 for
the HTML. The *button()* function is where *jQuery UI* comes in. It renders
our object as a jQuery UI button (see Figure 19). We then define what will
happen when the user clicks the button by defining its *click* function. We
call the *showO365Window* method, passing in the URL and the name of
the window. Within this function, we call the JavaScript *window.open()*
method with the URL, window name, and other attributes like the width
and height. The nice thing about using the window name is that the
browser will reuse that window if the user clicks the button again. If we use
_blank instead, then each time the user clicks the button, the browser will
create another window.

Listing 4. HTML for jQuery UI Button example

```
<div id="MainPageLinkButtons">
    <ul>
        <li>
            <button id="Google" class="O365Buttons" aria-
            label="Google" title="Google">Google</button>
        </li>
        <li>
            <button id="LinkedIn" class="O365Buttons" aria-
            label="LinkedIn" title="LinkedIn">LinkedIn</button>
        </li>
        <li>
            <button id="FaceBook" class="O365Buttons" aria-
            label="FaceBook" title="FaceBook">FaceBook</button>
        </li>
        <li>
            <button id="Twitter" class="O365Buttons" aria-
            label="Twitter" title="Twitter">Twitter</button>
        </li>
        <li>
            <button id="Bing" class="O365Buttons" aria-
            label="Bing" title="Bing">Bing</button>
        </li>
        <li>
            <button id="Microsoft" class="O365Buttons" aria-
            label="Microsoft" title="Microsoft">Microsoft
            </button>
        </li>
    </ul>
</div>
```

The HTML is pretty straightforward. As described previously, the styles (Listing 2) prevent the normal bullets from showing up for the *ul* and *li* items. The class of *O365Buttons* gives all the buttons a consistent width. The *aria-label* and *title* attributes handle the tooltip and ensure that accurate information is given to a screen reader (for accessibility). The JavaScript, jQuery, and jQuery UI (Listing 3) handle the functionality and styling.

jQuery UI has other useful widgets, but one other that we will demonstrate is the dialog. It is good for help information and disclaimers. At the Air Force Academy, we have a *Contact* link at the bottom of every page that gives an email link and phone number for assistance. Figure 20 shows an example but with a button instead of a link. Clicking the *Contact* button brings up the associated dialog. As with other examples, we load the styles, JavaScript, and HTML into a text file (Listing 5) and load it with a *Content Editor*.

Figure 20. *jQuery UI Dialog example page*

Listing 5. Style, JavaScript, and HTML for jQuery UI Dialog

```
<style>
    #contactdialog {
        display: none;
    }
</style>
```

```
<script src="https://code.jquery.com/jquery-3.3.1.min.js"></
script>
<script src="https://code.jquery.com/ui/1.12.1/jquery-ui.js"></
script>
<link rel="stylesheet" type="text/css" href="https://code.
jquery.com/ui/1.12.1/themes/redmond/jquery-ui.css">

<script type="text/javascript">
    $(function () {
        $("#contactlink").button().click(function () {
            $("#contactdialog").dialog({
                width: 500,
                buttons: [
                    {
                        text: "OK",
                        click: function () {
                            $(this).dialog("close");
                        }
                    }
                ],
            });

            return false;
        });
    });
</script>

<button id="contactlink" aria-label="Contact"
title="Contact">Contact</button>

<div id="contactdialog" title="Contact Support">
    <h2>Support Point of Contact:</h2>
    <br />
```

```
<h3>PHONE</h3>
<p>
    (719) 555-5555
</p>
<h3>
    E-MAIL
</h3>
<p>
    <a href="mailto:support@support.com">support@support.
    com</a>
</p>
</div>
```

The *style* is simple here. The *display: none;* just hides the element (div) that we will use for the dialog. We then link in the same jQuery and jQuery UI scripts and styles as in the previous example. We use the *button()* method to skin the button and define its *click* method as we did before. But now we get a reference to our *contactdialog* div and call the jQuery UI *dialog* method on it. It has a number of parameters to include *width* and *buttons* (just and *OK* button in this case that we use to close the dialog[1]). We return *false* from the function to prevent SharePoint for reloading its page (and closing the dialog before we ever see it).

The HTML consists of our *button* and our *div*. Notice that anything we put within the div will show up in the dialog.

---

[1]Notice the use of the *this* keyword to reference the dialog in the *$(this). dialog(close);* line. $(*this*) is the same in this context as $(*"#contactdialog"*).

CHAPTER 5

Customizing an Announcement List with jQuery

In this example, leadership wanted to have information about network alerts on our main SharePoint home page. At the Air Force Academy, we have two different networks (educational and military). Each alert would be characterized by order of importance as *Outage, HAZCON,* or *Informational.* My design was to have an *Announcements* list with unique permissions so that only the group that was allowed to add alerts could edit it. Everyone would have read access.[1] I would customize the display using jQuery so that outages would be more prominent.

The first step is to add two *Choice* columns: *Affected Network* and *Status.* These are shown in Figure 21.

---

[1]This is important. In my first release of this functionality, I had locked the list down so much that only myself and my initial testers could read the list. When my squadron director looked at it, he got an error message. I first thought there was a problem with the JavaScript but I eventually realized it was a permissions problem.

© Jeffrey M. Rhodes 2019
J. M. Rhodes, *Creating Business Applications with Office 365*,
https://doi.org/10.1007/978-1-4842-5331-1_5

Title *   SharePoint Down for Maintenance

Body   SharePoint will be unavailable this Thursday night from 2200 until
                         0500 Friday morning.

Expires   5/4/2018

Affected Network *   Both EDU and MIL

Status *   1. Outage
                         2. HAZCON
                         3. Informational   Save   Cancel

Figure 21. *Adding an alert with Choice columns*

We then add a *Calculated* column called *Alert*. Our objective is to
insert unique text that we can find with jQuery. We will determine the
Status from this unique text, use it to set the appropriate class, and then
remove the unique text. Figure 22 shows how you build the formula =" | | | "
& Status & " | | | " & Title. Following languages like Visual Basic, the &
symbol concatenates the pipe text with the values of the *Status* and *Title*
columns. For example, the alert in Figure 21 would have this value: *| | | 1.
Outage| | |SharePoint Down for Maintenance.* Don't click the box to *Add
to the default view* since we don't want users to see this text if they come to
the list page.

Formula: Insert Column:
                                  Affected Network
="|||"&Status&"|||"&Title   Compliance Asset Id
                                  Created
                                  Expires
                                  Modified
                                  Status
                                  Title

                                  Add to formula

Figure 22. *Calculated column for use by jQuery*

Next, we create two views: *EDUNotExpired* and *MILNotExpired*. As
shown in Figure 23, both show only the *Alert* and *Body* columns. They sort
by *Status* and then by *Title*. To avoid expired alerts, we only include items

where the expires is later than *[Today]*.[2] Finally, we only include items where the *Affected Network* contains *EDU*.[3] The *MILNotExpired* view is identical except we include items where the *Affected Network* contains *MIL*.

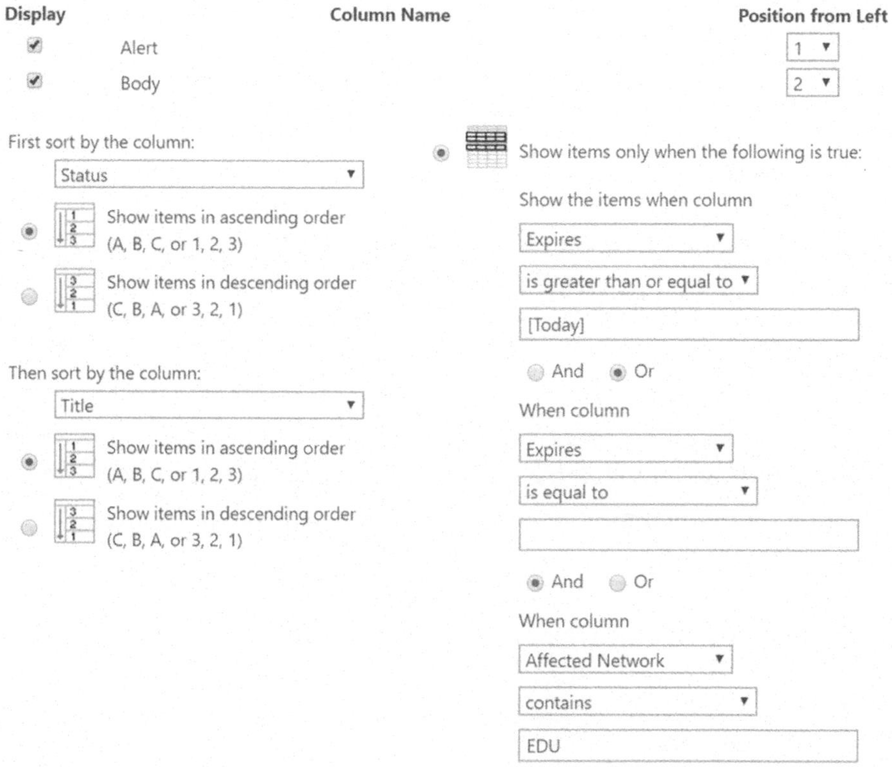

Figure 23. *EDUNotExpired view showing Columns, Sort, and Filter*

Our next step is to add two versions of list to a page as web parts. We set the view of the first one to *EDUNotExpired* and the second one as *MILNotExpired*. Figure 24 shows how it looks so far.

---

[2]Using *[Today]* in SharePoint filters is a powerful feature that I use often.
[3]Notice how the use of *contains* allows us to pick up items where the *Affected Network* is *EDU* as well as the ones where it is *both EDU and MIL*.

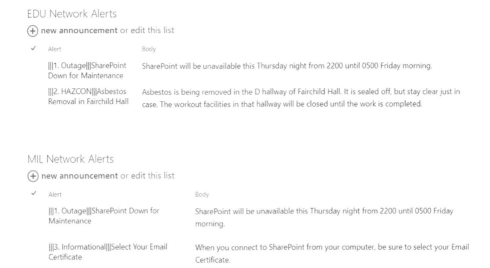

Figure 24. *Network Alerts web parts before adding jQuery*

As in the previous chapter, we save our styles and code to a text file, upload it into a document library, get the path to it, and link a *Content Editor* web part to it.

Listing 6. Styles for formatting Network Alerts

```
<style>
    .AlertOutage {
        font-weight: bold;
        font-size: 130%;
        color: red;
        padding-left: 5px;
    }

    .AlertHAZCON {
        font-weight: bold;
        font-size: 120%;
```

```
        color: #e5c636;
        padding-left: 5px;
    }

    .AlertInformational {
        font-size: 100%;
        color: blue;
        font-weight: bold;
        padding-left: 5px;
    }

    .USAFAOperational {
        color: #69aa39;
        font-size: 110%;
        font-weight: bold;
    }

    .ms-viewheadertr {
        display: none !important; /* prevents display of row
        with alert and body headings */
    }

    .TopPadding {
        padding-top: 20px;
    }
</style>
```

Listing 6 shows the part of the text file containing the style information. The gist of the logic is that the JavaScript (Listing 7) looks for text like *|||1. Outage|||* (see Figure 24) and uses that to apply the associated class (*AlertOutage* in this case) to the text. It then deletes this text, leaving just the title. Figure 25 shows the results for Outages, HAZCON, and Informational alerts. Notice how the class defines the color as well as the size and weight (bold).

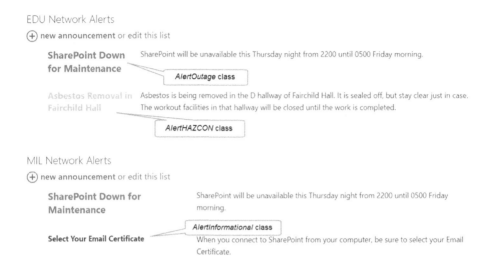

Figure 25. *Network Alerts showing the AlertOutage, AlertHAZCON, and AlertInformational classes*

To understand the next style, we need to look at what happens when there are no matching alerts. As shown in Figure 26, SharePoint automatically displays this text: *There are no items to show in this view of the "Network Alerts" list.*

Figure 26. *"No Items..." display and associated row id*

This isn't exactly what we want as this is not understandable to the customer. Instead, we want to replace this text and then format it green with the *USAFAOperational* class. But how do we find this text? Again, the Developer Tools come to the rescue. Figure 26 shows us that the row containing this text has an id[4] of *empty-WPQ4*. As we will see in Listing 7, we used that both the set to the style and to find the text and update it. Figure 27 shows the result.

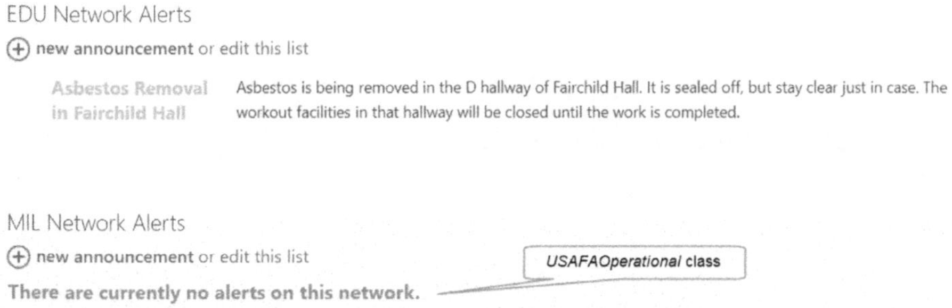

EDU Network Alerts

⊕ new announcement or edit this list

Asbestos Removal   Asbestos is being removed in the D hallway of Fairchild Hall. It is sealed off, but stay clear just in case. The
in Fairchild Hall   workout facilities in that hallway will be closed until the work is completed.

MIL Network Alerts

⊕ new announcement or edit this list   USAFAOperational class

There are currently no alerts on this network.

Figure 27. *Updated "No Item" text and associated USAFAOperational class*

If you look back at Figure 24, you might notice that there is a heading for the two columns that we are displaying in our view: *Alert* and *Body*. We want to eliminate those as well. As is a pattern now, we dig into the Developer Tools and see if we can figure out a way to do this.

---

[4]This is rare good news when using jQuery with SharePoint. As you may notice in other examples, we typically have to use classes and loop through them because the generated HTML does not often have ids. We are not totally out of the woods since it is possible for both lists to have empty elements, which then results in one row having a different id. But testing revealed that the id always started with *empty-WPQ*. Listing 7 shows actual jQuery logic.

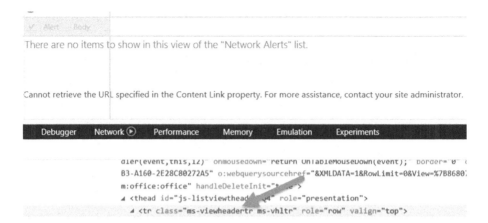

Figure 28. *Column heading and associated HTML via Developer Tools*

Since we want to hide the entire row, Figure 28 gives us a good clue. The table row (*tr*) has a class of *ms-viewheadertr*. Doing some searching for this class through the HTML of the page confirms that this class is only present on the rows that we want to hide. That allows us to take care of the issue for both alert lists with this line in the styles: *display: none !important;*. The *!important* keyword tells the browser for this definition to override others on the page. The final class, *TopPadding*, just gives us some improved formatting. The JavaScript/jQuery implementation is shown in Listing 7.

Listing 7. JavaScript for formatting Network Alerts

```
<script src="https://code.jquery.com/jquery-3.3.1.min.js">
</script>

<script>
    $(function () {
        var statusArray = ["1. Outage", "2. HAZCON",
        "3. Informational"];
        var statusLength = statusArray.length;
```

```
var num;
var status;
var fullStatus;
var className;

// look for all td elements containing |||1. Outage|||,
    etc.
$("td.ms-cellstyle.ms-vb2").each(function () {
    var currentText = $(this).text();

    for (num = 0; num < statusLength; num++) {
        status = statusArray[num];
        fullStatus = "|||" + status + "|||";
        className = "Alert" + status.substring(3);

        if (currentText.indexOf(fullStatus) > -1) {
            var newText = currentText.
            replace(fullStatus, ");
            $(this).html(newText);
            $(this).addClass(className);
        }
    }
});
$("tr.ms-alternating.ms-itmHoverEnabled > td").
addClass("TopPadding");
// account for no items
$("tr[id*='empty-WPQ'] > td").each(function () {
    $(this).html("There are currently no alerts on this
    network.");
    $(this).addClass("USAFAOperational");
});

    });
</script>
```

We start by again linking in the jQuery library. All the rest of our processing happens once the page is fully loaded.[5] We then define some key variables. You'll note that *statusArray* contains the possible status values from our list. We store its length as well, so we don't have to calculate it each time we iterate through our tables. The rest of the variables are used in the code that follows.

Our first challenge is getting our hands on our outage text such as *|||2. HAZCON|||*. Figure 29 shows that the best approach is to use the combination of the *ms-cellstyle* and *ms-vb2* classes. The *$("td.ms-cellstyle. ms-vb2")* selector means "find me all the td (table column) elements that have both the *ms-cellstyle* and the *ms-vb2* classes."[6] Note that it is possible that other web parts on the page not related to these alerts use these classes. But we loop through all of them on the page using jQuery's *each* function. We grab each one's *text()* and store it in the *currentText* variable. We then do a standard loop through our *statusArray*, add the pipes[7] (*|||*), and put the value in the *fullStatus* variable. While we are there, we build the *className*[8] in case we find a match. We use the JavaScript *indexOf* method to see if *currentText* contain *fullStatus*. If so, we use the *replace* function to create the *newText* variable with all the existing text except the part with the pipes and status (you might refer to Figure 24 to see how the alerts looked before running this script). We use the very handy jQuery *html* method to update the cell with the updated text. Finally, we use the jQuery *addClass* method to set the class to the corresponding value defined in Listing 6.

---

[5]As we have seen earlier, the shorthand for this is the *$(function () {}* syntax.

[6]The . means class.

[7]We use the pipes to avoid the possibility that other text on the page might match our code. *1. Outage* is possible on the rest of the page. *|||1. Outage|||* is not very likely to occur in other text.

[8]Notice how we use the *substring* function to get rid of the numbers at the front. So *className* will be a value like *AlertOutage*.

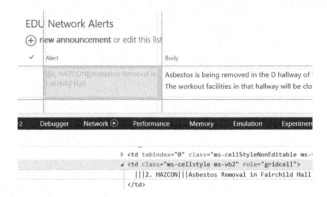

Figure 29. *Table column identified by ms-cellstyle and ms-vb2 classes*

Our next set of code looks for the rows between each entry and adds our *TopPadding* class to it.

Our final set of code addresses the "No Items" text and associated HTML shown in Figure 26. This selector is a bit complicated: *$("tr[id*='empty-WPQ'] > td")*. This means that we are looking for a table row when the id contains[9] the string *empty-WPQ*. Once we find that, find the *child* table column (td). From there, we again use the *html* method to update the text to "There are currently no alerts on this network." and the class to *USAFAOperational*. See Figure 27 for the results.

_____

[9]The * means contains in jQuery.

CHAPTER 6

Creating a Color Calendar

Keeping with our theme of improving out interface with JavaScript and jQuery, this example demonstrates how to create a color-coded calendar.[1] In this implementation, we take a single column,[2] display it with pipes (|||), and then use JavaScript/jQuery to color-code it (and remove the pipes).[3]

---

[1]The blog that I used as a basis for this approach is no longer available, but this thread links to it: `https://social.technet.microsoft.com/Forums/ie/en-US/b54640e8-0755-4ce0-ad95-26c3084decc0/sharepoint-2013-colour-coded-calendar.`

[2]Usually you want this to be a *Choice* column so that you can account for all the possible values. In general, I prefer *Lookup* columns so that you can put all the choices in a SharePoint list. But this solution requires a calculated column, and SharePoint doesn't allow you to get at the contents of a *Lookup* column from a formula. This also prevents you from allowing multiple values in the *Choice* column. I've worked around both of these issues by creating a workflow that automatically copies the value from the lookup column to another column, but that adds extra complexity.

[3]You can also create color-coded calendars using overlays. I find them less flexible and you have the risk of either losing or duplicating events as you create views for each color.

© Jeffrey M. Rhodes 2019
J. M. Rhodes, *Creating Business Applications with Office 365*,
https://doi.org/10.1007/978-1-4842-5331-1_6

In our example, we will create an *Event Location* column. Each location will have its own color. Once we create a new calendar or identify an existing calendar, we create a new *Choice* column described in footnote 2. I've named it *Event Location*[4] in Figure 30. Notice how we display choices with *Checkboxes* in order to allow multiple values.

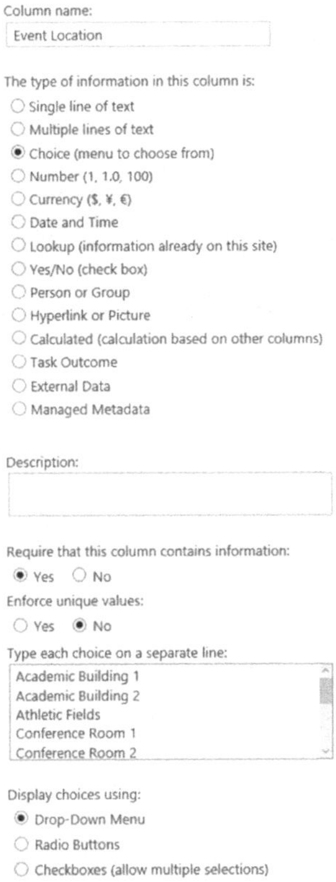

Column name:

Event Location

The type of information in this column is:

○ Single line of text
○ Multiple lines of text
◉ Choice (menu to choose from)
○ Number (1, 1.0, 100)
○ Currency ($, ¥, €)
○ Date and Time
○ Lookup (information already on this site)
○ Yes/No (check box)
○ Person or Group
○ Hyperlink or Picture
○ Calculated (calculation based on other columns)
○ Task Outcome
○ External Data
○ Managed Metadata

Description:

Require that this column contains information:
◉ Yes   ○ No

Enforce unique values:
○ Yes   ◉ No

Type each choice on a separate line:

Academic Building 1
Academic Building 2
Athletic Fields
Conference Room 1
Conference Room 2

Display choices using:
◉ Drop-Down Menu
○ Radio Buttons
○ Checkboxes (allow multiple selections)

Figure 30. *Event Location Choice column*

---

[4]We can't use the existing *Location* column since it is only a *Single line of text* column and SharePoint doesn't allow you to change its type. We will hide this column instead.

To avoid confusing the user, we want to hide the built-in *Location* column. We do this by clicking the *Event* Content Type.[5] Then click *Location* and choose for it to be *Hidden* as shown in Figure 31. We could also change the order of the columns if desired.

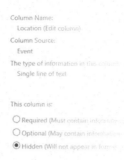

Figure 31. *Hiding the Location column*

Our next step is to create a *Calculated* column that we will use to create our colors. Since we want to be able to find our location programmatically (and not have any false positives where we change other elements on the page), we use three pipes (| | |). Here is our formula: "|||" & [Event Location] & "|||" & [Title]. As we say previously, this syntax concatenates the pipes with the column values (represented by the [Event Location] and [Title][6]). Figure 33 shows the creation on the *LocationTitle* calculated column.[7]

---

[5]If you are unable to edit the Content Type, click *Advanced settings* and choose *Yes* for *Allow management of content types?*.

[6]SharePoint also puts in the [] when you use the editor to build the formula. But they are optional if the column name does not have any spaces in it.

[7]A good technique is to copy your formula into a text editor like Notepad before clicking OK on your column. That way, a syntax error in your formula doesn't force you to recreate the whole formula.

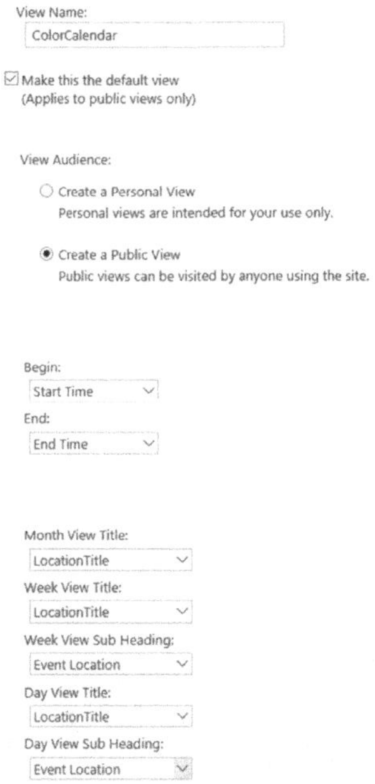

Figure 32. *The ColorCalendar view*

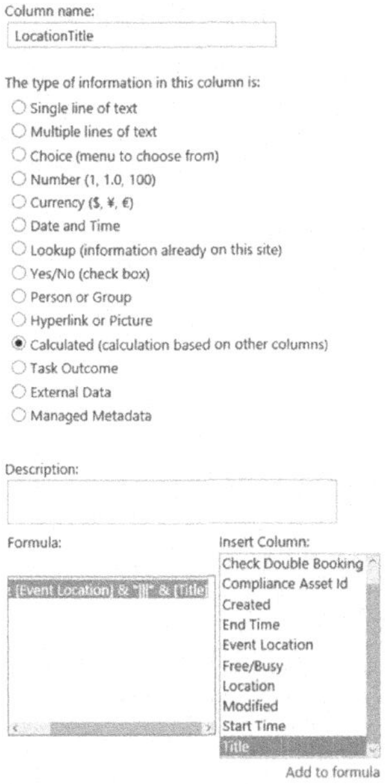

Figure 33. *The LocationTitle Calculated column*

We now need to create a special view that we will use for our color calendar. We choose a *Calendar View* and then configure it as shown in Figure 32. We basically just replace *Title* with *LocationTitle* and *Location* with *Event Location*. We check to *Make this the default view*. Figure 34 shows the results so far.

Figure 34. *Calendar display before adding JavaScript/jQuery*

We are now ready to add some code. As we did in Chapter 3 (refer to Figure 15), we put our code into a text file, upload it into a document library, and then link to it from a *Content Editor* web part. Listings 8 and 9 contain our code for implementing the color-coding.

Listing 8. JavaScript for color-coding the calendar – Part 1

```
<script src="https://code.jquery.com/jquery-3.3.1.min.js">
</script>

    <script type="text/javascript">
        var shouldColorText = true;
        var numUSAFAIterations = 0;
        var maxUSAFAIterations = 20;
        var SEPARATOR = "|||";

        $(function () {
            window.setTimeout(ColorCalendar, 1000);
        });
```

```
function ColorCalendar() {
    var container = $('#s4-bodyContainer');
    var query = 'a:contains(\" + SEPARATOR + '\')';

    numUSAFAIterations++;

    if (container.find(query).length > 0) {
        container.find(query).each(function (i) {
            var box = $(this).parents('div[title]');
            var colors = GetColorCodeFromLocation(GetLo
            cation(this.innerHTML));
            var anchor = $(this);

            anchor.text(GetActualText(anchor.text()))
            box.attr("title", GetActualText(box.
            attr("title")));
            box.css('background-color', colors[0]);
            box.css('display', 'block');
            if (shouldColorText) {
                box.find('div, a').css("cssText",
                "color: " + colors[1] +
                " !important;");
            }
        });
    }
    if (numUSAFAIterations <= maxUSAFAIterations) {
        window.setTimeout(ColorCalendar, 2000);
    }
}
```

As in earlier examples, we begin by linking in the jQuery library. We then define some variables. One of the challenges is that we can't fully predict when SharePoint will display all the calendar events. So we use JavaScript timers instead. Once the page is fully loaded (the jQuery *$(function())*, we use the *window.setTimeout()* function to call the *ColorCalendar()* function in 1 second (1000 milliseconds). Within that function, we get a reference to the *s4-bodyContainer* object and then look for an *anchor* that contains our pipes (*SEPARATOR* variable). Figure 35 makes that clearer using the *Developer Tools*. The arrows point to the two objects with the *anchor* for a particular event marked with a rectangle.

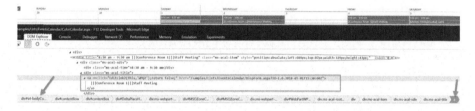

Figure 35. *Developer Tools showing the s4-bodyContainer and anchor*

We use the jQuery *each* method to loop through each anchor and then find the *parent* div that has a title (circled with the title of "8:30 am – 9:30 am …" in Figure 35). From there, we pass the innerHTML of the anchor[8] to the *GetLocation()* method, which is then passed to the *GetColorCodeFromLocation()* method, both of which are included in Listing 9. In our example, the InnerHTML is |||Conference Room 1|||Staff Meeting. As discussed in more detail in the following, *GetActualText()* returns Staff Meeting while *GetLocation()* returns Conference Room 1 in our example. We set the text of the anchor to *Staff Meeting* and set the *title* of the *box* to be that as well. We use our *colors*

---

[8]Figuring out what *this* refers to can be challenging. In this case, it is what came back from the *find* method, which is the anchor.

array to set the background and foreground colors appropriately using the jQuery *css* method. To keep the code from running forever, we stop it after 20 (*maxUSAFAIterations*) times.

Listing 9. JavaScript for color-coding the calendar – Part 2

```
function GetActualText(originalText) {
    var parts = originalText.split(SEPARATOR);
    var returnString = parts[2];

    return returnString;
}

function GetLocation(originalText) {
    var parts = originalText.split(SEPARATOR);

    return parts[1];
}

function GetColorCodeFromLocation(location) {
    var locationArray = location.split(",");
    var bgcolor = '#4802fb';
    var fgcolor = '#ffffff';

    switch (location.trim()) {
        case 'Academic Building 1':
            bgcolor = '#cd0000';
            fgcolor = '#ffffff';
            break;
        case 'Academic Building 2':
            bgcolor = '#eb8f0b';
            fgcolor = '#000000';
            break;
```

```
case 'Gym':
    bgcolor = '#ffff00';
    fgcolor = '#000000';
    break;
case 'Conference Room 1':
    bgcolor = '#0a4723';
    fgcolor = '#ffffff';
    break;
case 'Conference Room 2':
    bgcolor = '#3d1c45';
    fgcolor = '#ffffff';
    break;
case 'Football Stadium':
    bgcolor = '#45aff2';
    fgcolor = '#000000';
    break;
case 'Gym':
    bgcolor = '#4169e1';
    fgcolor = '#ffffff';
    break;
case 'Headquarters':
    bgcolor = '#790bf3';
    fgcolor = '#ffffff';
    break;
case 'Library':
    bgcolor = '#000000';
    fgcolor = '#ffffff';
    break;
case 'Not Applicable':
    bgcolor = '#f0cb20';
    fgcolor = '#000000';
    break;
```

```
        case 'Off Base':
            bgcolor = '#838785';
            fgcolor = '#ffffff';
            break;
        case 'Theater':
            bgcolor = '#731717';
            fgcolor = '#ffffff';
            break;
    }
    return [bgcolor, fgcolor];
}
```

In *GetActualText*, we pass in the calculated title (such as
|||Conference Room 1|||Staff Meeting). We use the JavaScript *split*
command to create an array, which looks like this:

```
parts[0] = ""
part[1] = "Conference Room 1"
parts[2] = "Staff Meeting"
```

Since what we want back is the actual title of the event, we send back
parts[2]. We do the same thing in *GetLocation*, but now we want the
location and send back *parts[1]*. In *GetColorCodeFromLocation*, we pass in
this location and return an array of the background color and foreground
color. We saw back in Listing 8 how we then used that to set the colors of
the boxes. You can look ahead to Figure 36 to see the result.

We are not quite finished, however. We would like to have a legend so
that the user knows the meaning of each color. We use a similar technique
as mentioned earlier where we upload *CalendarLegend.txt*, which is
shown in Listing 10, add a *Content Editor* web part, and link it to this file.

Listing 10. Calendar legend styles and HTML

```
<style >
#CalendarLegend ul {
      list-style: none;
}

      #CalendarLegend ul li {
            display: inline-block;
            padding: 3px;
      }

#CalendarLegend span {
      width: 250px;
      color: white;
      display: block;
      text-align: center;
      font-size: 125%;
      font-weight: bold;
}

#AcademicBuilding1 {
      background-color: #cd0000;
}

#AcademicBuilding2 {
      background-color: #eb8f0b;
      color: black !important;
}

#AthleticFields {
      background-color: #ffff00;
      color: black !important;
}
```

```
#ConferenceRoom1 {
        background-color: #0a4723;
}

#ConferenceRoom2 {
        background-color: #3d1c45;
}

#FootballStadium {
        background-color: #45aff2;
        color: black !important;
}

#Gym {
        background-color: #4169e1;
}

#Headquarters {
        background-color: #790bf3;
}

#Library {
        background-color: #000000;
}

#NotApplicable {
        background-color: #f0cb20;
        color: black !important;
}

#OffBase {
        background-color: #838785;
}

#Other {
```

```
        background-color: #4802fb;
}

#Theater {
        background-color: #731717;
}
</style >
<div id="CalendarLegend">
        <ul>
            <li><span id="AcademicBuilding1"> Academic
            Building 1</span></li>
            <li> <span id="AcademicBuilding2"> Academic
            Building 2</span> </li>
            <li><span id="AthleticFields"> Athletic Fields
            </span></li>
            <li> <span id="ConferenceRoom1"> Conference Room
            1</span> </li>
            <li> <span id="ConferenceRoom2"> Conference Room
            2</span> </li>
            <li> <span id="FootballStadium"> Football Stadium
            </span> </li>
            <li> <span id="Gym"> Gym</span> </li>
            <li> <span id="Headquarters"> Headquarters</span>
            </li>
            <li> <span id="Library"> Library</span> </li>
            <li> <span id="NotApplicable"> Not Applicable
            </span> </li>
            <li> <span id="OffBase"> Off Base</span> </li>
            <li> <span id="Theater"> Theater</span> </li>
            <li> <span id="Other"> Other</span> </li>
        </ul>
    </div>
```

We use the HTML unordered list (*ul* and *li* tags) to create our legend. This allows them to wrap to the available space. These would normally display as bullets, but we use styles to set the *list-style* to *none*, the *display* to *inline-block,* and their *padding* to 3 pixels. We set the *span* within them to be a particular width, font, alignment, and so on. Note how the *color* is defined as *white*. The rest of the styles match up to the location name (with any spaces removed). They define the corresponding background color (that matches that in Listing 9). If the text needs to be black instead (e.g., if the background is a light color), then the color style is set with the *!important* attribute to override the span's style.

Figure 36 shows the final result. When it comes time to use these files for a new calendar, you can open an editor like Visual Studio and do a search and replace for location names across both of these files.

Figure 36. *Completed legend and color calendar*

What if we want to show the color calendar on another page? That is pretty straightforward. We add the calendar as a web part, change its view to the same *ColorCalendar* view created previously, and then add two *Content Editor* web parts and link them to the same code and legend text files.

CHAPTER 7

Preventing Double-Booking of Calendar Events

The genesis of this chapter was a request by our Registrar for a solution so that cadets scheduling tutor appointments would be prevented from trying to book an appointment that overlaps another tutoring session.[1] Each tutor has his or her own SharePoint calendar. They had a solution in our previous SharePoint 2010 version, but that involved "Resource Reservations" and was deprecated in SharePoint 2013. I found some references to a JavaScript/jQuery solution, which as you can probably already tell were much more up my alley. In this solution, we check any existing regular or recurring appointments before accepting a new or edited appointment. If the new or edited appointment overlaps an existing appointment, the user is shown a message and the appointment does not go through. Note that this approach checks against existing recurring appointment but does NOT check a new recurring appointment against conflicts. So new recurring events could overlap either other recurring appointments or existing regular appointments.

---

[1]This solution also prevents appointments being scheduled when the tutor is on vacation or otherwise out of the office, assuming those events are added in the calendar.

© Jeffrey M. Rhodes 2019
J. M. Rhodes, *Creating Business Applications with Office 365*,
https://doi.org/10.1007/978-1-4842-5331-1_7

The implementation steps are pretty straightforward. We use *SharePoint Designer* to copy these three files to the same location as the calendar:

- jquery.js (jquery-3.3.1.min.js in our example)

- checkRecurringEvents.js

- checkDoubleBook.js

- jquery.SPServices-2014.02.min.js

checkRecurringEvents.js is a somewhat customized version of the code listed and explained at `https://anvlpopescu.wordpress.com/2014/09/06/get-calendar-recurrent-events-with-caml`. Thanks go to Popescu Andrei Vlad for the excellent code and making it available for reuse. Here are the credits and licensing for the jquery.SPServices-2014.02.min.js file:

```
/*
 * SPServices - Work with SharePoint's Web Services using
   jQuery
 * Version 2014.02
 * @requires jQuery v1.8 or greater - jQuery 1.10.x+
   recommended
 * Copyright (c) 2009-2014 Sympraxis Consulting LLC
 * Examples and docs at:
 * http://spservices.codeplex.com
 * Licensed under the MIT license:
 * http://www.opensource.org/licenses/mit-license.php
 */
/* @description Work with SharePoint's Web Services using
   jQuery
 * @type jQuery
 * @name SPServices
```

```
 * @category Plugins/SPServices
 * @author Sympraxis Consulting LLC/marc.anderson@
   sympraxisconsulting.com
*/
```

Again, thanks go to Marc Anderson and Sympraxis Consulting for creating such a useful library.

We use Designer's *Import Files* button or just drag and drop our files to the same location as the calendar's *NewForm.aspx* and *EditForm.aspx* as shown in Figure 37.

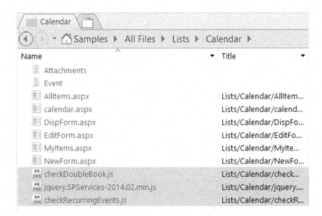

Figure 37. *Copying checkDoubleBook.js, jquery.SPServices-2014.02. min.js, and checkRecurringEvents.js to the location of Calendar forms*

Our next step is to edit *checkDoubleBook.js*. We next need to put the name of the calendar into this file. It is important to use the actual name as opposed to the URL. The distinction is that the URL will never change but the list name can be edited. For example, if we first create a calendar with the name *XYZ*, its URL will be <site url>/Lists/XYZ/calendar.aspx. If we then go to *List Settings ➤ List name, description, and navigation* and change the name to *PDQ*, the URL will not change. But we need to use *PDQ* in this example in our *checkDoubleBook.js* file.

We either *Edit File in Advanced Mode* in Designer as shown in Figure 38 or edit the file in another program before copying it with Designer. We then look for this line and make sure it matches the current name of the calendar:

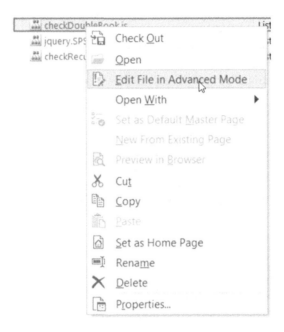

Figure 38. *Editing checkDoubleBook.js in SharePoint Designer*

```
Var listName = 'Calendar';
```

Our next step is to again Edit File in Advanced Mode with EditForm. aspx and NewForm.aspx.[2]

Look for this line in both files:

```
<asp:Content ContentPlaceHolderId="PlaceHolderMain" runat="server">
```

---

[2]It is possible to change the name of these forms in Designer. You can go to *Lists and Libraries,* click the name of the calendar, and then look at the *Forms* area of the page to see if the names of the *Edit* or *New* forms have a different name.

Put these lines directly below that line. Note that the order of the lines is important.

```
<script src="https://code.jquery.com/jquery-3.3.1.min.js"
type="text/javascript"></script>
<script src="jquery.SPServices-2014.02.min.js" type="text
/javascript"></script>
<script src="checkRecurringEvents.js" type="text/javascript">
</script>
<script src="checkDoubleBook.js" type="text/javascript">
</script>
```

Figure 39 shows how it looks in Designer.

```
14  <asp:Content ContentPlaceHolderId="PlaceHolderMain" runat="server">
15  <script src="https://code.jquery.com/jquery-3.3.1.min.js" type="text/javascript"></script>
16  <script src="jquery.SPServices-2014.02.min.js" type="text/javascript"></script>
17  <script src="checkRecurringEvents.js" type="text/javascript"></script>
18  <script src="checkDoubleBook.js" type="text/javascript"></script>
19  <SharePoint:UIVersionedContent UIVersion="4" runat="server">
20      <ContentTemplate>
21      <div style="padding-left:5px">
22      </ContentTemplate>
```

Figure 39. *Adding the JavaScript files to EditForm.aspx and NewForm.aspx using SharePoint Designer*

Figure 40 shows the result when a user tries to add or edit an appointment that conflicts with either a regular or recurring[3] event. This event is squarely in the middle of another event, but for testing we need to try the boundary conditions like overlapping by 1 minute, scheduling back-to-back appointments, and trying in different browsers.[4]

---

[3]The recurring appointments cause some extra work as described in the following, but the additional effort is worth it because recurring events like staff meetings, lunch times, and workouts are very common.

[4]We will see in the following code that we needed to account for different time zones. This came out when my initial solution worked in Internet Explorer but not Chrome.

As mentioned previously, what does NOT work is conflicts between a new recurring event and any existing events in the calendar. That may be possible, but the complexity was not worth it for this situation.

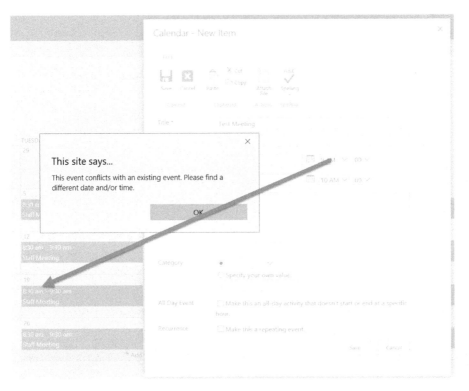

Figure 40. *Message showing that the prevention of a double-booked calendar appointment. Notice that the conflict is with a recurring appointment*

Let's look at the code itself.[5] This solution uses SharePoint's JavaScript Object Model. `https://docs.microsoft.com/en-us/sharepoint/dev/sp-add-ins/complete-basic-operations-using-javascript-library-code-in-sharepoint` has some additional information. The standard

---

[5]Feel free to skip this next part if *how* this all works is not of great interest.

model has the capability to query the calendar for standard events in order to detect overlaps. However, it doesn't allow the developer to query *recurring* events for other than the current year, month, or day. To check for recurring events in the future, we need to call SharePoint's web services. Listing 11 shows the initial part of *checkDoubleBook.js*.

Listing 11. Part 1 of checkDoubleBook.js

```
var saveBtn;
var saveBtnCallbackId;
var listName = 'Calendar';
var conflictString = "This event conflicts with an existing
event. Please find a different date and/or time.";
var startDate;
var startDateTime;
var endDate;
var endDateTime;
var currentTimeZoneOffset = "-06:00";

// unbind click handler for Save button
$(function () {
    saveBtn = $("[id*='diidIOSaveItem']");
    if (saveBtn) {
        saveBtnCallbackId = saveBtn.attr("name");
        saveBtn.unbind('click').click(checkForOverlaps);
    }
});

// override default action
function PreSaveItem() {
    return false;
}
```

```
function checkForOverlaps() {
    var txtDateStart = $("[title='Start Time Required Field']");
    var txtDateEnd = $("[title='End Time Required Field']");
    var cboHoursStart = $("#" + $("label:contains('Start Time
    Required Field Hours')").attr("for"));
    var cboMinutesStart = $("#" + $("label:contains('Start Time
    Required Field Minutes')").attr("for"));

    if ((txtDateStart.length > 0) && (txtDateEnd.length > 0) &&
    (cboHoursStart.length > 0) && (cboMinutesStart.length > 0)) {
        var dateValStart = txtDateStart.val();
        var hoursValStart = formatHours(cboHoursStart.val());
        var minValStart = cboMinutesStart.val();
        var cboHoursEnd = $("#" + $("label:contains('End Time
        Required Field Hours')").attr("for"));
        var cboMinutesEnd = $("#" + $("label:contains('End Time
        Required Field Minutes')").attr("for"));
        var dateValEnd = txtDateEnd.val();
        var hoursValEnd = formatHours(cboHoursEnd.val());
        var minValEnd = cboMinutesEnd.val();
        var startDateString = dateValStart.concat(" ").concat
        (hoursValStart).concat(":").concat(minValStart);

        startDate = new Date(startDateString);
        startDateTime = startDate.getTime();

        var offset = startDate.getTimezoneOffset();
        var offsetInHours = (offset / 60);

        currentTimeZoneOffset = "-0" + offsetInHours + ":00";

        var endDateString = dateValEnd.concat(" ").concat
        (hoursValEnd).concat(":").concat(minValEnd);
```

```
        endDate = new Date(endDateString);
        endDateTime = endDate.getTime();

        currentId = getCurrentId();

        Shp.Lists.getMonthEvents(listName, startDate,
        querySucceeded);
    }
    else {
        saveCustomAction();
    }
}

function getCurrentId() {
    var returnVal = null;
    var regex = new RegExp("[\\\?&]" + "ID" + "=([^&#]*)");
    var qs = regex.exec(window.location.href);

    if (qs != null) {
        returnVal = qs[1];
    }

    return returnVal;
}

function formatHours(hoursVal) {
    // if 12-hour format, hoursVal will look like this: 11 AM
    // if 24-hour format, hoursVal will look like this: 17:
    var hoursArray;

    if (hoursVal.indexOf(":") > -1) {
        hoursArray = hoursVal.split(":");
    }
    else {
        hoursArray = hoursVal.split(" ");
    }
```

```
    var returnHours = (hoursArray[0] - 0);

    if (hoursArray[1] == "PM") { // only relevant for 12-hour
                                    regional setting format.
        if (returnHours < 12) { // leave alone for 12 PM
            returnHours = returnHours + 12;
        }
    }
    else {
        if (returnHours == 12) {
            returnHours = 0; // 12 AM needs to be 00
        }
    }

    return returnHours;
}
```

We start with various global variables that we will use throughout the file. Next, we again use the jQuery *document.ready* functionality (shorthanded to *$(function () {});* to override the functionality of the *Save* button on the form. We basically tell it to call our *checkForOverlaps* function instead of its normal built-in operation. How do we find the *Save* button? We use the *Developer Tools* as shown in Figure 41. Looking closely at the *id* attribute, we see that it contains *_diidIOSaveItem*. We use this in the selector line *saveBtn = $("[id*='diidIOSaveItem']");*. While we are there, we notice that the *onclick* event calls *PreSaveItem,* and if that returns *true*, call the *WebForm_DoPostBackWithOptions* function. Very importantly, it sends a long parameter that ends up being the *name* attribute.

Figure 41. *Developer Tools showing how the id for the Save button contains _diidIOSaveItem and how the name is used for the onclick event*

Getting back to the *checkDoubleBook.js* code, we store this *name* attribute for later and *unbind* the *click* event and instead call our *checkForOverlaps*. Next, we return *false* from *PreSaveItem* to ensure that the original Save button code doesn't get called.

The idea behind *checkForOverlaps* is that we need to get our hands on the start date/time and end date/time of the proposed event. We then compare those to existing events in the calendar. The initial challenge is to read the dates and times from the form. We again use *Developer Tools* to inspect the rendered HTML and come up with the best strategy. Figure 42 shows how the *title* attribute allows us to get our hands on the date portion of the *Start Time*. That is the basis of this line:

```
var txtDateStart = $("[title='Start Time Required Field']");
```

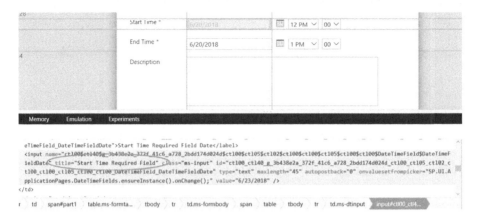

Figure 42. *Developer Tools showing how the title attribute allows us to select the starting date*

We use the jQuery *val()* method to read what the user entered or selected in the date and time boxes. For the hours, we use a *formatHours* function to account for formatting differences (e.g., it could be 5 PM or 17). It is easiest to use a 24-hour clock, so we add 12 to the hour value if we detect PM in the value.[6] We then need to merge all these values into a JavaScript date object. We build *startDateString* with a value like "6/26/2018 8:00." That allows us to initialize a date object (*startDate*). We then use the JavaScript *getTime()* method to convert the date to the number of milliseconds since 1970. The makes our date comparisons easier. We do the same thing with the end date. While we are at it, we store our *currentTimeZoneOffset*, which is the difference from Greenwich Mean Time. We will use this later. Next, we need to account for the difference between a new and edited event. When we edit an event, the SharePoint web service will give us the current version of this event. So we don't want

---

[6]You might notice this line in *formatHours*: *var returnHours = (hoursArray[0] - 0);*. This is a common technique to account for the fact that JavaScript does not have defined types like number or string. To ensure that the browser interprets *returnHours* as a number, we subtract 0 from it. Otherwise, we can get situations where a line like *returnHours + 12* would give a value like "512" rather than 17.

to conflict with ourselves. So we need to skip any comparison to this exact same event. We do this by storing the *currentId*. We get this by looking at the URL of the Edit or New form. Here is how it looks for an edit:

```
https://plattecanyon.sharepoint.com/samples/Lists/Calendar/
EditForm.aspx?ID=3&Source=https%3A%2F%2Fplattecanyon%2Esharepoi
nt%2Ecom%2Fsamples%2FLists%2FCalendar%2Fcalendar%2Easpx
```

The part we want (ID=3) is in bold. The *getCurrentId* function uses regular expressions to grab this value. The New form does not have this ID value. Finally, we call the *checkRecurringEvents.js* file with this line:

```
Shp.Lists.getMonthEvents(listName, startDate, querySucceeded)
```

We pass in the *listName* ("Calendar" in our example), the *startDate* JavaScript date object, and the function to call upon successful completion, *querySucceeded*. Listing 12 shows the most important parts of *checkRecurringEvents.js*, which is based on Popescu Andrei Vlad's code as mentioned previously. I made some adjustments for Chrome to account for events spanning multiple days and using the *getTime()* method for data comparisons.

Listing 12. Key parts of checkRecurringEvents.js

```
var Shp = Shp || {};

Shp.Lists = {};

Shp.Lists.getMonthEvents = function (list, date, callback) {
    var calendarDate = new Date(date.getFullYear(), date.
    getMonth(), 15);
    var checkDateTime = calendarDate.getTime();
    var month = date.getMonth();
    var year = date.getFullYear();
    var day = date.getDate();
```

```
var caml = "<Query>" +
                        "<Where>" +
                              "<DateRangesOverlap>" +
                                    "<FieldRef Name=
                                    'EventDate' />" +
                                    "<FieldRef Name=
                                    'EndDate' />" +
                                    "<FieldRef Name=
                                    'RecurrenceID' />" +
                                    "<Value Type=
                                    'DateTime'
                                    IncludeTimeValue=
                                    'FALSE'>" +
                                    "<Month />" +
                                    "</Value>" +
                              "</DateRangesOverlap>" +
                        "</Where>" +
                        "<OrderBy>" +
                              "<FieldRef Name=
                              'EventDate' />" +
                        "</OrderBy>" +
                  "</Query>";

jQuery().SPServices({
    operation: 'GetListItems',
    async: true,
    listName: list,
    CAMLQuery: caml,
    CAMLRowLimit: 100,
```

```
CAMLQueryOptions: '<QueryOptions><DateInUtc>FALSE
</DateInUtc><ViewAttributes Scope="RecursiveAll" />
<CalendarDate>' + Date.toISOFormat(calendarDate) +
'</CalendarDate><IncludeMandatoryColumns>TRUE</IncludeM
andatoryColumns><RecurrencePatternXMLVersion>v3
</RecurrencePatternXMLVersion><ExpandRecurrence>TRUE
</ExpandRecurrence></QueryOptions>',
completefunc: function (data, status) {
    if (status === 'success') {
        var events = Shp.Lists._serializeResponse(data.
        responseXML);
        var items = [];
        for (var i = 0; i < events.length; i++) {
            var start = events[i].get_item('EventDate');
            var end = events[i].get_item('EndDate');

            if (isInRange(start) === true
            || isInRange(end) === true ||
            isInDuration(start, end) === true) {
                items.push(events[i]);
            }
        }
        callback(items);
    }
    else {
        alert("Error in reading events for calendar '"
        + list + ".' Please check that the calendar has
        not been renamed.");
    }
}
});
```

```
    function isInRange(dateString) {
        var dt = dateString.split(' ')[0];
        var dateArray = dt.split('-');
        var y = parseFloat(dateArray[0]);
        var m = parseFloat(dateArray[1]) - 1;
        var d = parseFloat(dateArray[2]);
        var inRange = (y === year && m === month && d === day);

        return inRange;
    }

    function isInDuration(startDateString, endDateString) {
        startDateString = startDateString.replace(" ", "T");
        // put in 2015-07-29T13:00:00 format
        endDateString = endDateString.replace(" ", "T");
        // put in 2015-07-29T13:00:00 format

        var startDate = new Date(startDateString);
        var endDate = new Date(endDateString);
        var startDateTime = startDate.getTime();
        // milliseconds since 1970
        var endDateTime = endDate.getTime();
        var inDuration = ((startDateTime <= checkDateTime) &&
        (endDateTime >= checkDateTime));

        return inDuration;
    }
}

Shp.Lists._serializeResponse = function (xml) {
    var items = new Array();
    var rows = xml.getElementsByTagName("z:row");
```

```
    if (rows.length == 0){ //Chrome
        rows = xml.getElementsByTagName("row");
    }

    for (var i = 0; i < rows.length; i++) {
        items.push(new Shp.ListItem(rows[i]));
    }
    return items;
}
```

The key to this functionality is using the *Collaborative Application Markup Language (CAML)*[7] and SharePoint's exposed web services to query the calendar for its existing events. After creating some date variables in the *getMonthEvents* function, we build the *caml* variable. Those of you familiar with *Standard Query Language (SQL)* will notice some similarities. Most important for our purposes are the *DateRangesOverlap* and *Month* tags. The *caml* tells SharePoint to give us the Event (Start) date, end date, and id for all values within a given month, ordering by the Event date. We then use *jQuery.SPServices* file to call SharePoint's *GetListItems* web service function. In addition to passing in the name of the calendar, the query, and the fact that we want an asynchronous call, we give it *CAMLQueryOptions*. This includes the proposed event date and the *ExpandRecurrence*, which tells SharePoint to include all the recurring events. The web service returns *data* and *status*. If the *status* is success,[8] we use the *_serializeResponse* function to parse the values into a JavaScript *events* object. We read the *start* and *end* objects and

---

[7]See https://msdn.microsoft.com/en-us/library/office/ms467521.aspx for details on CAML.

[8]The main reason that I've found for it NOT to return success is when the end user renames the calendar without changing the *checkDoubleBook.js* file. That's why the error message displays the expected name of the calendar and asks to check if it has been renamed.

then do some rough checking (we do more detail later) to see if the event starts on, ends on, or overlaps the day of our proposed event. If so, we add it to the *items* collection. This is shown in the *Developer Tools* in Figure 43.

Figure 43. *Developer Tools debugger showing the items collection that we pass to the callback function*

We then pass *items* back to the callback function, *querySucceeded*, which is shown in Listing 13.

Listing 13. Part 2 of checkDoubleBook.js

```
function querySucceeded(items) {
    // this returns both regular and recurring events that
        either begin or end on the start date
    // Note that it will not pick up multiday events that span
        this date
    var itemId;
    var id;
    var eventStartDate;
    var eventEndDate;
    var eventStartDateString;
    var eventEndDateString;
```

```
var eventStartDateTime;
var eventEndDateTime;
var startCalc1;
var startCalc2;
var endCalc1;
var endCalc2;
var hasConflict = false;

for (var i = 0; i < items.length; i++) {
    itemId = items[i];
    id = itemId.get_item("ID");

    if (currentId != id) { // can't conflict with ourself
        eventStartDateString = itemId.get_item("EventDate");
        eventEndDateString = itemId.get_item("EndDate");
        eventStartDateString = eventStartDateString.
        replace(" ", "T").concat(currentTimeZoneOffset);
        // put in 2015-07-29T13:00:00-7:00 format
        eventEndDateString = eventEndDateString.replace(" ",
        "T").concat(currentTimeZoneOffset);
        eventStartDate = new Date(eventStartDateString);
        eventEndDate = new Date(eventEndDateString);
        eventStartDateTime = eventStartDate.getTime();
        // milliseconds since 1970
        eventEndDateTime = eventEndDate.getTime();
        startCalc1 = (eventStartDateTime <= startDateTime);
        startCalc2 = (startDateTime < eventEndDateTime);
        // not <= since can start at the same time as the
        end of the previous event
        endCalc1 = (eventStartDateTime < endDateTime);
        // not <= since the previous event can end at the
        start time of this event
        endCalc2 = (endDateTime <= eventEndDateTime);
```

```
            hasConflict = (startCalc1 && startCalc2) ||
            (endCalc1 && endCalc2) || (startCalc2 && endCalc1);

            if (hasConflict) {
                break;
            }
        }
    }

    if (hasConflict) {
        alert(conflictString);
    }
    else {
        saveCustomAction();
    }
}

function saveCustomAction() {
    WebForm_DoPostBackWithOptions(new WebForm_PostBackOptions
    (saveBtnCallbackId, "", true, "", "", false, true));
}
```

We start in *querySucceeded* by declaring all the variables we need.
We then loop through the *items* returned from the web service. We
grab each one's *ID* so that we can compare it to the *currentId* variable.
If they match, then we stop comparing since this is the event we are
editing. Otherwise, we use the *get_item* method to get our hands on the
EventDate and *EndDate*. We put it in the current format, including the
currentTimeZoneOffset discussed earlier, so that we can create a new
JavaScript date object. We get convert it to milliseconds from 1970 using
the *getTime()* method. We now can do our calculations comparing the start
and end of the two events. The *hasConflict* variable is *true* if the proposed
event overlaps the existing event in any way. In that case, we display the

warning message and stop comparing. If not, we check the rest of the events. If there are no conflicts, we call the *saveCustomAction*, which in turn makes this call:

```
WebForm_DoPostBackWithOptions(new WebForm_PostBackOptions(saveB
tnCallbackId, "", true, "", "", false, true));
```

Compare this to Figure 41. This is the original *onclick* call for the Save button, making use of our *saveBtnCallbackId* variable that we grabbed initially.

CHAPTER 8

Building an Accordion Interface

A popular request at the Air Force Academy was a more elaborate "accordion" interface where information could be hidden until it was needed. I wanted to find a solution where non-web developers could create and, more importantly, maintain the pages. I liked the solution created by Patrick Abel and described at `https://info.summit7systems.com/blog/how-to-create-dynamic-accordions-in-sharepoint-pages`. I made some minor modifications to give the result shown in Figure 44.

Figure 44. *Accordion page showing collapsed Documents, Calendar, and FAQ sections*

© Jeffrey M. Rhodes 2019
J. M. Rhodes, *Creating Business Applications with Office 365*,
https://doi.org/10.1007/978-1-4842-5331-1_8

Rather than embed the code on the page as referenced in the blog posting, I used our now-familiar technique of putting the code in a text file and referencing it in a Content Editor as shown in Figure 45. Notice how we set the *Chrome Type* to *None*. This means that the Title (Accordion Code – Do Not Delete) will only be shown when the page is being edited.

Figure 45. *Content Editor referencing Accordion code*

For users, it is easy to create the sections. They just set whatever text they want to be a section as *Heading 1*. We can see this in Figure 46.

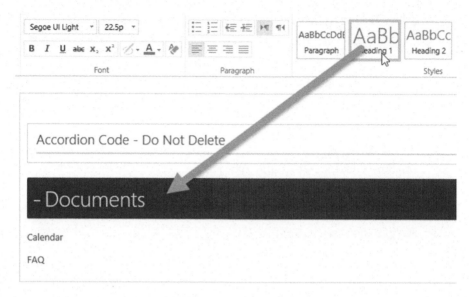

Figure 46. *Setting an Accordion section by setting its style to Heading 1*

Let's first look at the styles (Listing 14). We take advantage of the fact that the main divider in a SharePoint page has the id of *DeltaPlaceHolderMain*. We then define any *h1* tag[1] within that div with the desired color, rounding, cursor, and so on. This is the expanded color with a blue background (#002b5c). When we look at the JavaScript (Listing 15), we will see that it dynamically adds or removes the *expand* class when the user clicks the heading. That swaps the background (gray #e4e5e6) and text color to show the expanded state. The *content* reflects a + for collapsed and a – for expanded.[2]

---

[1]If you compare this to Patrick's blog, you'll see that I used *h1* rather than *h2*, mainly so that the sections would be bigger.

[2]I removed the specialty *FontAwesome* font since our machines had problems displaying this font.

Listing 14. The style section of accordionDesign.txt

```
<style type="text/css" >

/*** CSS for collapsible headers ***/
#DeltaPlaceHolderMain h1 {
      background: #002b5c;
      padding: .25em;
      border-radius: 2px 2px 2px 2px;
      color: #e4e5e6;
      cursor: pointer;
      margin-bottom: .5em;
}

#DeltaPlaceHolderMain h1.expand {
      background: #e4e5e6;
      color: #002b5c;
}

#DeltaPlaceHolderMain h1.expand:before {
          content: '\002B ';
          padding-right: 5px;
          font-weight: bold;
      }
/*** Expanded h1 ***/
#DeltaPlaceHolderMain h1:before {
      content: '\002D ';
      padding-right: 5px;
      font-weight: bold;
}

</style >
```

Listing 15 shows the accordion logic.

Listing 15. The JavaScript section of accordionDesign.txt

```
<script src="https://code.jquery.com/jquery-3.3.1.min.js">
</script>

<script type="text/javascript">

var collapseHeaders = true; // added functionality so headers
                               are not automatically collapsed
                               unless set to true -- JMR
// from http://info.summit7systems.com/blog/how-to-create-
dynamic-accordions-in-sharepoint-pages

Sys.WebForms.PageRequestManager.getInstance().add_
pageLoaded(MyPageLoaded);
function MyPageLoaded(sender, args) // use this instead of
                                       document.ready since
                                       calendars fully loaded
                                       by this event
{
    UpdateToggle();
}

function UpdateToggle(){
    var inEditMode = Utils.checkPageInEditMode();
    // Prevent the collapsing of <h1> blocks when in
       SharePoint's [Edit Mode]
    if (!inEditMode) {
        UI.collapseContentHeaders();
        UI.toggleContentHeaders();
    }
}
```

```
var UI = {
    collapseContentHeaders: function () {
        $('#DeltaPlaceHolderMain h1').each(function (index,
        value) {
            // Collapses all <h1> blocks except for the first
                encountered
            if ((index > 0) && collapseHeaders) {
                $(this).toggleClass('expand').nextUntil('h1').
                slideToggle(100);
            }
        });
    },
    toggleContentHeaders: function () {
        // Toggles the accordion behavior for <h1> regions onClick
        $('#DeltaPlaceHolderMain h1').click(function () {
            $(this).toggleClass('expand').nextUntil('h1').
            slideToggle(100);
        });
    }
}

var Utils = {
    checkPageInEditMode: function () {
        var pageEditMode = null;
        var wikiPageEditMode = null;
        // Edit check for Wiki Pages
        if (document.forms[MSOWebPartPageFormName]._wikiPageMode) {
            wikiPageEditMode = document.forms
            [MSOWebPartPageFormName]._wikiPageMode.value;
        }
```

```
    // Edit check for all other pages
    if (document.forms[MSOWebPartPageFormName].MSOLayout_
    InDesignMode) {
        pageEditMode = document.forms
        [MSOWebPartPageFormName].MSOLayout_InDesignMode.value;
    }
    // Return the either/or if one of the page types is
       flagged as in Edit Mode
    if (!pageEditMode && !wikiPageEditMode) {
        return false;
    }
    return pageEditMode == "1" || wikiPageEditMode == "Edit";
    }
}
</script>
```

We start with the *collapseHeaders* variable, which allows us to easily control whether the headers start all collapsed. Some users wanted them to be collapsed while others didn't. We then use SharePoint's *PageRequestManager* to call our *MyPageLoaded* function once the page is completely loaded. As mentioned in the comment, this is better than jQuery's *document.ready* function in this case since calendars can take some time to load and we need to wait until they are done before trying to create the accordions. This *UpdateToggle* function first sees if we are in editing mode of the page. It does this by calling the appropriately named *checkPageInEdit* mode function.[3] This uses some specialized knowledge

---

[3]Notice how this function is a property of the *Utils* object. This is often done to prevent conflicts between different JavaScript libraries. If we defined *checkPageInEdit* mode as function right in the page, there might be different library that has a function of the same name. Here we can only get a conflict if two libraries have the same object name AND function name. We do this again shortly with the *UI* object.

of SharePoint Wiki and normal pages to determine if a user is editing the page. If we are editing, we don't do anything else. This allows us the ability to work with the page and define our accordion sections. Otherwise, we call two more functions of our *UI* object: *collapseContentHeaders* and *toggleContentHeaders*.

In *collapseContentHeaders*, we again use the jQuery *each* function to find every *h1* block inside the *DeltaPlaceHolderMain* div. We leave the first div expanded (which is why we have *index > 0*). We also check that our *collapseHeaders* variable is true. *$(this)* is a jQuery object referring to the div in question. We then call the *toggleClass* method, which adds the class if it is not there and removes if it is. Since the page is just being loaded, the class is not there. As we saw in Listing 14, the *#DeltaPlaceHolderMain h1.expand* class defines the background as gray and the color as a dark blue. The *#DeltaPlaceHolderMain h1.expand:before* selector puts all the items (a + symbol [represented in Unicode 002B], padding, and bold) immediately before the item. The *nextUntil('h1')* method means to apply this until the next h1 element. *slideToggle(100)* applies the style with a slide animation that lasts 100 milliseconds. Look back at Figure 44 to see how the collapsed sections look.

In *toggleContentHeaders*, we turn on the ability to collapse and expand the sections. It defines the *click* handler on all the headers.[4] It just calls the same *toggleClass* method described in the previous paragraph. When the *expand* class is removed, then the *h1* style is used, which is a blue background. The *h1:before* selector kicks into place, which prepends the + symbol. Figure 46 shows how this looks.

---

[4]*$('#DeltaPlaceHolderMain h1')* is a selector for all h1 elements within the div with an ID of "DeltaPlaceHolderMain."

CHAPTER 9

Creating an Approval Process with Microsoft Flow

New to Office 365 is Microsoft Flow, which makes it easier to create workflows. It will work across Office 365, but we will concentrate on its use in SharePoint and Forms.

For our example, we will create an *Equipment Request* list as shown in Figure 47. We add columns for the submission date, required date, manager name and email,[1] cost, and so on. We use *Microsoft Flow* to get approval from the manager and, if approved, email the purchasing manager.

---

[1]We could just have the manager be a *Person* column and use that email, but my thought was to allow emails out of the SharePoint system (e.g., to a Gmail account). As discussed in the following, this is not working for me in Office 365.

© Jeffrey M. Rhodes 2019
J. M. Rhodes, *Creating Business Applications with Office 365*,
https://doi.org/10.1007/978-1-4842-5331-1_9

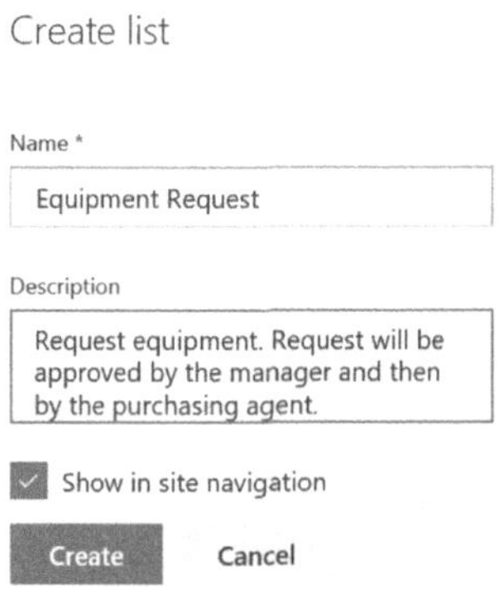

Create list

Name *

Equipment Request

Description

Request equipment. Request will be
approved by the manager and then
by the purchasing agent.

☑ Show in site navigation

Create   Cancel

Figure 47. *Custom Equipment Request list*

Figure 48 shows the steps. We *Create a flow* from the *Flow* menu and
select the choice to *Start approval when a new item is added*. We then
select the flow, noting that it involves *SharePoint, Approvals*, and *Outlook*.
Creating the flow itself is like filling out a form. We select the list name
and then *Add dynamic content* for selecting who the approval should be
assigned to. Note how we choose the *Manager Email* column from our list.
Upon approval, we first email the purchasing manager, including various
information such as the title, required date, approver, any comments, and
the link to the request.

Note that the email address for the *Approval* steps needs to be
associated with a user within SharePoint.[2] Other emails (such as to the
purchasing manager) do not cause an error when going to an outside
address.

---

[2]For example, it works when I use my *onMicrosoft.com* address but fails when I
use my normal email address. Here is the error message in that case: The request
failed. Error code: *'InvalidApprovalSubscribeRequestAssignedToMissing.'* Error
*Message: 'Required field 'assignedTo' is missing, empty, or contained no valid
users.'*. SharePoint 2013 workflows have a similar issue. We launch SharePoint 2010
workflows to send emails outside of the one associated with a SharePoint user.

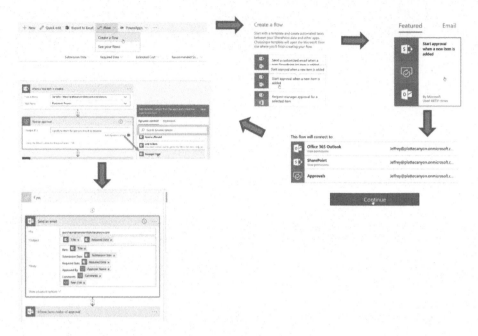

Figure 48. *Creating a list with an Approval flow*

Adding an item kicks off the flow. Figure 49 shows both the email to the manager requesting approval and the email received by the requester showing that the item has been approved.

Figure 49. *Approval emails from Microsoft Flow*

CHAPTER 10

Creating a Survey Response Dashboard with Microsoft Power BI

Power BI[1] is a powerful tool for visualizing data. Of particular relevance for this book is its ability to use SharePoint lists as a data source. In this chapter, we will demonstrate how to use Power BI to display SharePoint survey data. This is particularly useful for a long-running survey such as for a help desk. As shown in Figure 50, SharePoint's built-in graphical summary displays all results. If the survey has been in place for the past 5 years, seeing recent trends is impossible. In addition, there is no way to click the *Very Dissatisfied* responses, for example, and drill down into their comments or other information.

---

[1]Learn more at https://powerbi.microsoft.com.

© Jeffrey M. Rhodes 2019
J. M. Rhodes, *Creating Business Applications with Office 365*,
https://doi.org/10.1007/978-1-4842-5331-1_10

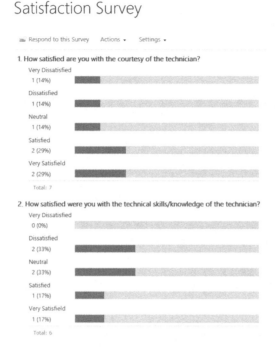

Figure 50. *SharePoint's graphical survey summary*

We will focus on the free *Power BI Desktop* application for this example, but you could publish to *Power BI Service* or *Power BI Report Server* as well if you have those products. To get started, we select *Get Data* in Power BI and choose *SharePoint List* or *SharePoint Online List*. We put in the path to our site (not including the survey itself). Power BI will prompt us to either use our current credentials or to log into our Microsoft account, as appropriate. It then allows us to select one or more lists as shown in Figure 51.

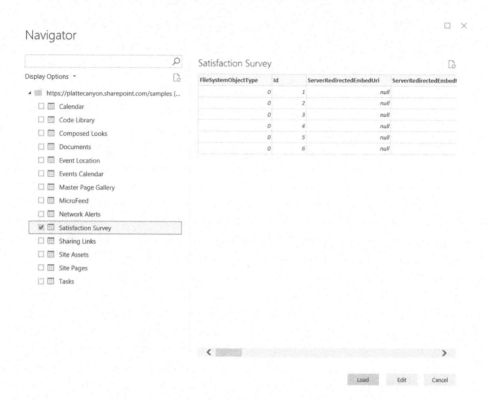

Figure 51. *Selecting a SharePoint survey in Power BI Desktop*

Our next step is to *Edit Queries* as shown in Figure 52.

Figure 52. *Edit Queries in Power BI Desktop*

Power BI gives us a nice interface to filter our data, rename columns, and much more. It shows all the actions in *APPLIED STEPS* so that we can view, edit, or remove them later (see Figure 54). Better yet, these steps are re-accomplished on the live data each time we refresh the data. You might notice in Figure 52 that the column names are truncated as in *How satisfied are_x0*. It will be most convenient to rename them to the full text of the associated question. To do that, we right-click the column and select *Rename*. We then copy in the full question from SharePoint.

Some of the columns are displayed as *Record* or *Table*. In that case, we click the button on the right side of the column as shown in Figure 53 to the right. We choose to include the *Name, FirstName,* and *LastName* columns.

Figure 53. *Expanding a Record column into individual elements*

To display responses that are within a specific range, it will be useful to create a column that shows the number of days between today's date and the data of the response. To do this, we go to the *Add Column* tab and then select *Custom Column*. We will name the column *DaysPassed* and use this formula:

```
DateTime.From(DateTime.LocalNow()) - [Modified] + #duration
(0, 6, 0, 0)
```

This gives the number of days since the survey was modified. We add 6 hours since in my case the Office 365 server is 6 hours later than my local time. Since we don't care about decimals, we *Change Type* of the column to a whole number. Figure 54 shows the result.

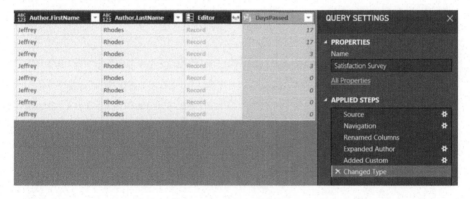

Figure 54. *Expanded and custom columns in Power BI Query Editor*

Now that we have the data like we want it, we are ready to make some visualizations. We go to the *Report* view and create a *pie chart* visualization. We drag the question into *Details* and then the *Id* column as the *Values* as shown in Figure 55. Power BI defaults to the *count* of the ID, which we then rename as responses. This then shows us the number of responses of each type (Satisfied, Dissatisfied, etc.).

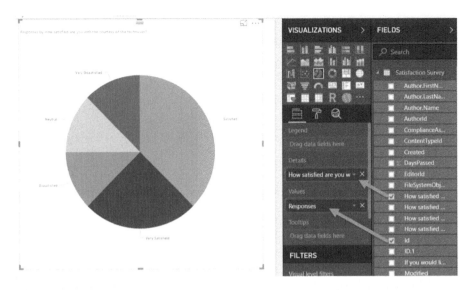

Figure 55. *Pie chart visualization in Power BI*

Rather than letting Power BI define the colors, we next go to *Format*
➤ *Data colors* to give our own colors for each of the response types.[2]
Figure 56 shows the results. We use a *Slicer* and connect it to the *Created*
date[3] (which we rename Survey Date). We use the *Table* visualization to
display detailed information such as the first and last name of the person
who filled out the survey.

---

[2]I prefer to go to Photoshop to find the color I want, grab that color in hexadecimal
format (such as 073f05 for *Very Satisfied*), and then paste that into Power BI.

[3]Power BI interprets the data type as *String*. You need to change it to *Date/Time* in
order for the slicer to display as slider as shown in Figure 56.

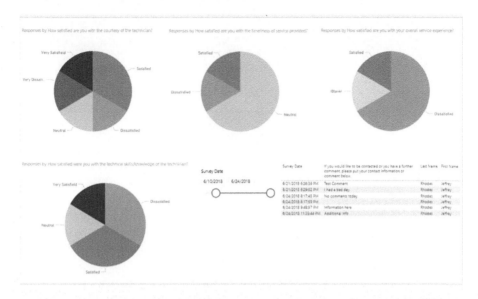

Figure 56. *Completed visualizations showing pie chart per question, slicer of the survey date, and table of additional information*

One of the most powerful features of Power BI is the ability to drill down into specific data. In Figure 57, we see the results of clicking the *Dissatisfied* result in the first question. The other questions adjust to how they were answered for the surveys that were dissatisfied for the first question. The table adjusts as well. The manager can then contact the customer to get more details and ensure the problem does not happen again.

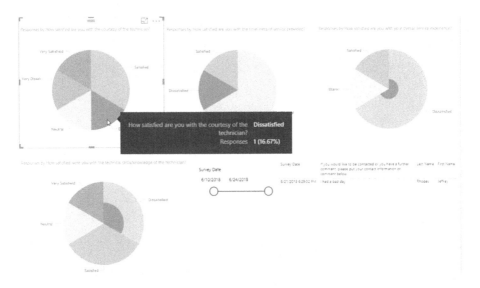

Figure 57. Drilling down on a Dissatisfied result in Power BI

If you have a Power BI online account, you can publish it via Power BI Desktop. It then displays in the browser as shown in Figure 58. This has the huge advantage of not requiring the installation of Power BI Desktop on each client machine.

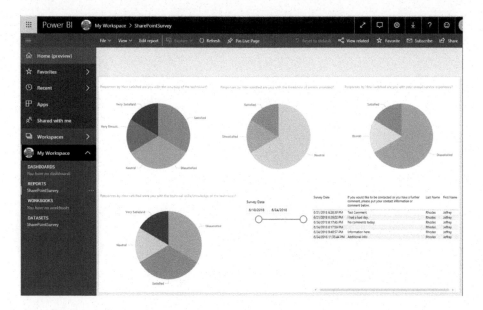

Figure 58. *Published Power BI report*

If you have the *Pro* version of Power BI, you can then embed the report directly in Office 365.[4] You copy the resulting URL and then add the *Power BI* app to a modern page (this doesn't work in a classic page) as shown in Figure 59.

Figure 59. *Embedding Power BI into a SharePoint modern page*

---

[4]See https://docs.microsoft.com/en-us/power-bi/service-embed-report-spo.

CHAPTER 11

Creating a Survey Solution with Microsoft Forms, Flow, SharePoint, and Power BI

An exciting new feature[1] of Office 365 is *Microsoft Forms*. While not yet as powerful as *InfoPath*, Forms makes it very easy to create forms and surveys. In this example, we will create a survey for our help desk in Forms (similar to what we did with a built-in SharePoint survey in the last chapter). Since we can't currently use Forms as a data source for Power BI, we will use *Flow* to copy each survey response to a SharePoint[2] list. We then use this SharePoint list as our Power BI data source.

---

[1]The availability of Microsoft Forms may depend on your Office 365 version. When I first created this chapter, Forms was not available in my personal version of Office 365 Professional but was part of our Office 365 Education at the Air Force Academy. When I checked back later, it had been added to Office 365 Professional as well.

[2]This has the added benefit of keeping a permanent record of the response. If someone deleted a survey response, the record of the response is still in SharePoint.

© Jeffrey M. Rhodes 2019
J. M. Rhodes, *Creating Business Applications with Office 365*,
https://doi.org/10.1007/978-1-4842-5331-1_11

Figure 60. *Sharing a form to allow anyone to respond*

One big advantage of Forms over SharePoint's built-in survey capabilities is the ability to allow anyone to respond. This is configured on the *Share* tab as shown in Figure 60. Figure 61 shows a section of a survey.

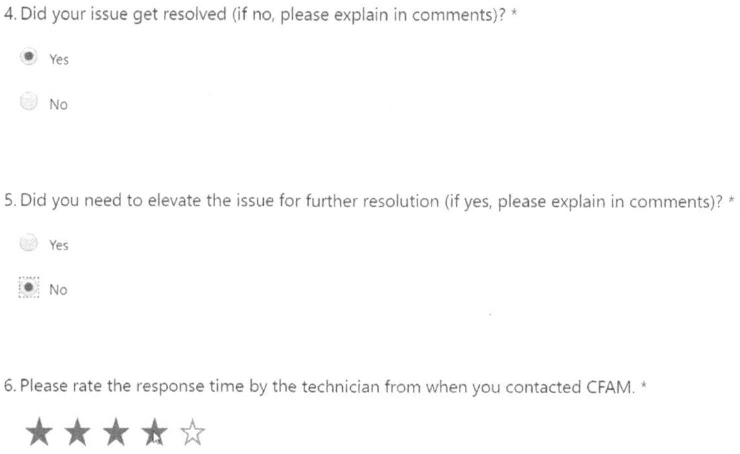

4. Did your issue get resolved (if no, please explain in comments)? *

   ◉ Yes

   ◌ No

5. Did you need to elevate the issue for further resolution (if yes, please explain in comments)? *

   ◌ Yes

   ◉ No

6. Please rate the response time by the technician from when you contacted CFAM. *

   ★ ★ ★ ★ ☆

Figure 61. *Microsoft Forms survey*

Notice that there is a built-in *Rating* question type where you can set the number of levels (the preceding *Rating* question type has five). Figure 62 shows the interface when you click the *Add Question* button. You can also choose to include a subtitle, make the question required, allow a "long answer" (for the *Text* question type), limit to a number or range (again for *Text*), and allow multiple answers, the "shuffling" of answers, and/or *Other* option (*Choice* type). Since we will automatically get the date when we add the response to SharePoint, I don't normally include a *Date* type unless I am looking for them to enter a date in the future such as the "required by" date.

Figure 62. *Microsoft Forms question type: Choice, Text, Rating, and Date*

Our next step is to create a list (Figure 63) in SharePoint for holding the data. I typically make all the columns *Single line of text* or *Multiple lines of text*.[3] This avoids data type problems when being transferred from Flow. We can fix the data types once we get to Power BI.

Issue Summary	Issue Resolved?	Issue Elevated?	Technician Respons...	Technician Knowled...	Customer Satisfacti...	Turnaround Time	Technician Courteous	Recommend CFAM	Comments
Computer problem	Yes	No	5	5	5	5	Yes	Yes	n/a now
Reset local admin password, install printer drivers	Yes	No	5	5	5	5	Yes	Yes	
WiFi Connection	Yes	No	5	5	5	5	Yes	Yes	
New CAC certificates	Yes	No	4	4	4	5	Yes	Yes	Most of the certificate issues were solved, but not all. This may be beyond the expertise of the CFAM people. But I did have to go down a second time as the first person didn't do all the...

Figure 63. *SharePoint list for holding the Forms survey data*

Within Flow, we create a new flow from a template and search for *SharePoint* as shown in Figure 64. We choose the one to *Record form responses in SharePoint*. From there, we pick the form and fill in each field in turn (Figure 65). Notice that the template includes the *Apply to each* action. If you were building this flow from scratch, you would need to add this action. We then select the SharePoint site and list that we want to populate. From there, we go to each list column and select the corresponding form entry. Note that the form questions are labeled by the text of the question. As many of these start with *Please rate...*, it is helpful to have the form open when doing this step.

---

[3]Be sure to use *Multiple lines of text* if more than 255 characters are possible, such as for a multiple response question like those shown in the next chapter.

Figure 64. *Searching for a SharePoint template to record form responses*

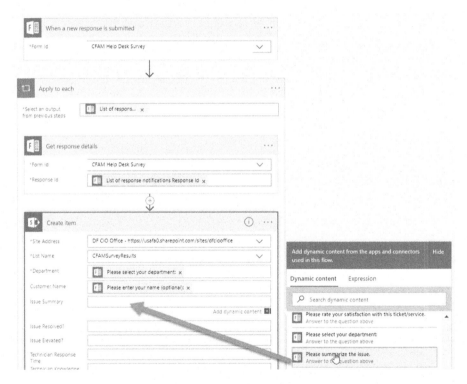

Figure 65. *Creating the flow to copy form responses to a SharePoint list*

Once you save the flow, fill out the form and then go to both Flow and SharePoint to see the results. If there are errors, Flow will give you the details.

From here, the task is very similar to the previous chapter, where we connected Power BI to a SharePoint survey. We again rename the columns as needed, since they are often truncated. We create a *DaysPassed* column with the formula =DateTime.From(DateTime.LocalNow()) - [Created]. This allows us to segregate responses into the week, month, quarter, and so on as shown in Figure 66. We also update the *Data colors* so that a low score (1) is red, a high score (5) is green, and the ones in between transition from orange to yellow to light green.

Figure 66. *Power BI showing survey results by date*

CHAPTER 12

Power BI Challenges with JSON, XML, and Yes/No Data

Adding in multiple answers, multiple lines of text, and Yes/No responses leads to some additional challenges. For example, we did an *IT Demographic Survey* of all our academic personnel at the Air Force Academy. I used the same technique as the previous chapter to copy each response to a SharePoint list using Microsoft Flow. We see the first inkling of an issue when we look at the data in SharePoint as shown in Figure 67. The extra explanatory text after *Level 4* gets copied (since it was part of the answer). More significantly, the multiple answers get represented as *["EDU (wired)", "MIL"]*. Those with some web programming experience might recognize this as *JavaScript Object Notation*. When we connect to the data in Power BI, we see an additional issue in that the data is displayed as HTML[1] as shown in Figure 68.

---

[1]This might not have happened if I had selected *Plain Text* in the SharePoint column properties, but users had already started responding to the survey by then.

© Jeffrey M. Rhodes 2019
J. M. Rhodes, *Creating Business Applications with Office 365*,
https://doi.org/10.1007/978-1-4842-5331-1_12

Figure 67. *Text and JSON data from Forms and SharePoint*

Figure 68. *HTML format in Power BI for multiline text in SharePoint*

The value looks like this:

```
<div class="ExternalClass32D98E29A2FB4239AA704C30B14455BC">
[&quot;Yes. The current visual projection capability in my
classroom is sufficient.&quot;]</div>
```

Since there are [] in the data as well, this is actually JSON data inside of HTML. This will affect our actions within Power BI.

As in the previous chapter, we connect to the SharePoint list as our data source and then *Edit Query* to begin manipulating the data. Our first task is to deal with *null* data. We initially sent out the survey requiring answers, but we updated it later for the stragglers with a request to just fill out the first four questions with the option to skip the rest. For those columns that were JSON or HTML, this meant that we needed put in *[]* for JSON data and *<div></div>* for HTML data. As discussed previously, for *both* JSON and HTML, we used *<div>[]</div>*. This is shown in Figure 69.

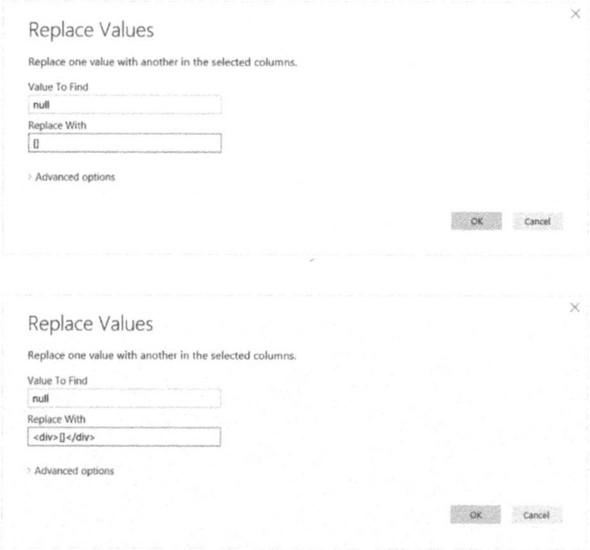

Figure 69. *Replacing null JSON and HTML/JSON values in Power BI*

Our next task is to remove all the extraneous text from our *IT Level* and instead have it show *Level 1* through *Level 4*. As shown in Figure 70, we use the *Extract* option and then use *First Characters*, which turns out to be seven. This will make our visualizations much cleaner.

Figure 70. *Extracting the first seven characters of the IT Level column*

We have two tasks when working with the JSON data. The first is to eliminate the brackets and the quotes. We do this by going to *Extract – JSON* as shown in Figure 71. The second task is more difficult. Notice how the first row contains *EDU (wired), MIL* while the second contains *EDU (wired), EDU (wireless)*. If we do a visualization "as is," one "pie slice" will be the *EDU (wired), MIL* combination and the other will be the *EDU (wired), EDU (wireless)* combination. What we actually want is to show two *EDU (wired)* answers and one each for *MIL* and *EDU (wireless)*. To make this happen, we need to split each response into its own row. As shown in Figure 72, we click the "Expand" button at the top of the column.[2] We then select *Expand to New Rows*.[3] Each entry gets its own row. Notice the circled *Id* values in Figure 72. These are duplicated and are how we will match up these extra rows to the original responses.

Figure 71. Parsing JSON data in a multiple response column

---

[2]Note how the previous step of parsing the JSON turned the values to *List* instead of text.

[3]We could also choose *Extract Values*. In that case, we would pick the delimiter (comma in this case) and then we could tell it whether to make rows or columns.

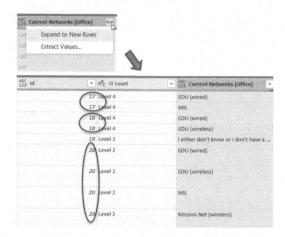

Figure 72. *Expanding multiple responses into separate rows*

We do this for each of the multiple response columns. In our example, we started with 270 rows of data. After expanding all the columns, we ended up with 1,227,676 rows! Luckily, Power BI can handle this extra data just fine.

The process for the HTML data is similar. We first note that HTML is a special case of eXtensible Markup Language (XML). We thus use the *Parse – XML* option as shown in Figure 73. Note how this operation converts the HTML into a *Table*. We then click the Expand button on the column and choose *Element:Text* to get our text data. As discussed previously, this turns out to be JSON data in our case. So we then *parse* and *expand* it like we did in Figure 71 and 72.

After performing these steps on all our JSON and XML columns,[4] we are ready to visualize the data. As we have seen in previous examples, we put the desired column (*Current Networks (Office)* in this case) as the *Details* and then find a unique value like *Id* for the *Count*. Figure 74 shows

---

[4]We also created a *DaysPassed* column as in past examples using the formula =DateTime.From(DateTime.LocalNow()) - [Created]. We can use this in future years to compare survey results over time.

the results. When we look at the tooltip showing the *# of Responses* for *EDU (wired)*, we see the problem. 308,753 responses reflect all the expanded rows described earlier in this chapter and does not reflect the true data.

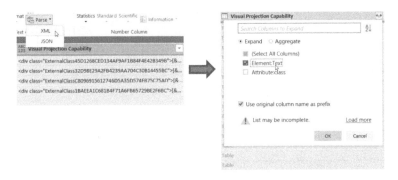

Figure 73. *Parsing XML and then selecting Element:Text*

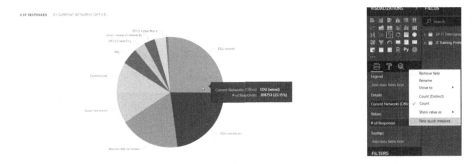

Figure 74. *Erroneous results when using Count*

We can now take advantage of the fact we noticed in Figure 72 that the *Id* values were duplicated when we expanded the rows. We use *Count (Distinct)* instead as shown in Figure 75. The *# of Responses* is now reasonable at 261. Notice how the percentage is much different as well.

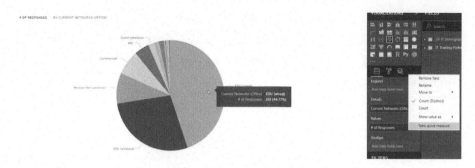

Figure 75. *Correct results when using Count (Distinct)*

Another implication of the expanded rows becomes apparent when we want to view the actual data. I normally use a *Table* for this purpose (refer back to Figure 56 for an example). If we do that here, however, we see all the duplicate data (name, department, IT Level, etc.). Instead, we can use a *Matrix* as shown in Figure 76. We add each desired element to *Rows* and then click the *Expand all down one level in the hierarchy* button (see arrow in Figure 76) until it is disabled. We then turn off *Stepped layout* under *Row headers*.

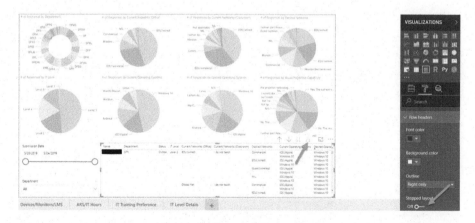

Figure 76. *Using a Matrix without stepped layout instead of a Table*

111

Our final task for this chapter is to effectively display Yes/No (or Boolean) data. Figure 77 shows a portion of our daily status check form. It is largely a series of Yes/No/Other questions on whether various systems and networks are operational.

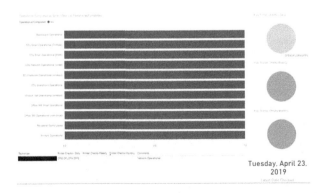

Figure 77. *Daily Check form showing Yes/No data*

While we could easily make a standard pie chart for each question showing the numbers of *Yes* and *No* responses, this doesn't give us the desired "dashboard" of both the most recent date (Figure 78) and the results over a given timeframe (Figure 79). To do this, we need to make some adjustments to the data.

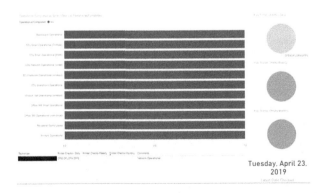

Figure 78. *Dashboard showing most recent Daily Check data*

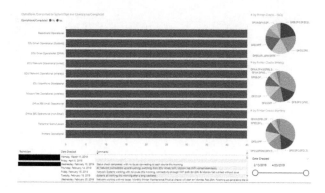

Figure 79. *Dashboard showing Daily Check data over time*

As with previous examples, we go to *Edit Queries.* Before we get into the Yes/No data, let's look at how we come up with the "Most Recent Date." We don't want to limit this to "today" since the daily check may not have occurred yet and we want to yesterday's (or Friday's if this a Monday) data. For this, I found the easiest way was to first create a *MostRecentSubmissionDate* column using this formula:

```
=List.Max(#"Changed Type"[Created])
```

This gives us a column that has the same value in every row, for example, *4/23/2019 1:34:33 PM.* We then add a *Conditional Column* that we name *isMostRecentDate.* We put *1* in this column if the *Created* column equals the *MostRecentSubmissionDate* and *0* if not. We change its type to *True/False* and then use it as the *page level filter* as shown in Figure 80. This limits all data on the page/tab to only the most recent.

Figure 80. *isMostRecentDate conditional column and associated page level filter*

Getting back to our Yes/No data, we remove all the unneeded columns (*Author, Editor,* etc. that came over from SharePoint). We then select all the Yes/No columns and choose to *Unpivot Only Selected Columns* as shown in Figure 81. This gives us a new *Attribute* column (that was the previous column name) and a new *Value* column (which is Yes/No/Other). We rename these to *System/Task* and *Operational/Completed,* respectively.

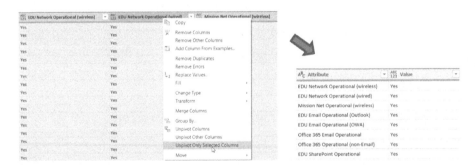

Figure 81. *Unpivoting Yes/No columns leading to Attribute and Value columns*

We are now ready to make our visualization. We choose *stacked bar chart* and use *System/Task* for the Axis, *Operational/Completed* as the Legend, and the Count of *Operational/Completed* as the Value. Since *Yes* is good and *No* is bad in our context, we set the *Data Colors* so that Yes is green and No is red. This is shown in Figure 82.

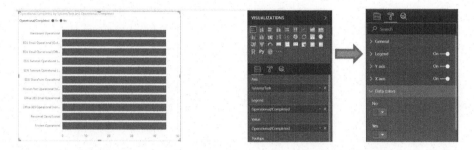

Figure 82. *Configuring the stacked bar chart to include custom data colors*

CHAPTER 13

Power BI Case Study: Monitoring BMC Remedy Help Tickets

Power BI can also be used for non-Office 365. An example that we have found helpful is in monitoring Remedy tickets. Remedy is an IT Service Management software that manages incidents, work orders, and other items. An important task is monitoring ticket status, how long they have been open, whether they have been assigned, and other tasks. Before Power BI, this had been accomplished by exporting data from Remedy to Excel and then creating charts. Not only was this labor-intensive, but the data was stale by the time it was presented at a staff meeting. Figure 83 shows one of our Power BI dashboards. It covers data from the previous 90 days and shows the number of tickets by support group (section), the status, the organization (Mission Element) with the issue, who submitted the ticket,[1] who the ticket was assigned to, and so on.

---

[1]As we will discuss later in the chapter, finding out the submitter for a ticket was a major issue. This was because technicians use their Common Access Card to log into the system. This in turn meant that the "login" info in Remedy was a number associated with this card. Going into the Remedy to view a ticket only showed this number. We fixed this with Power BI.

© Jeffrey M. Rhodes 2019
J. M. Rhodes, *Creating Business Applications with Office 365*,
https://doi.org/10.1007/978-1-4842-5331-1_13

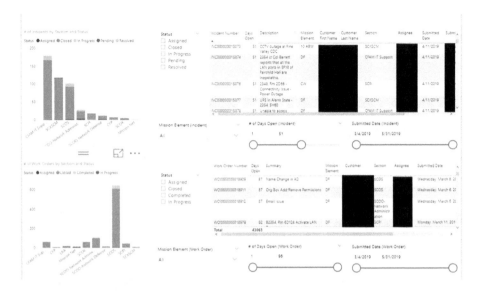

Figure 83. *Power BI dashboard showing Remedy ticket data*

Remedy did not expose a data source that could be used by Power BI, so I went straight to its database (Microsoft SQL Server in our case). It took some effort to find the right data, but eventually discovered that the BMC developers had created views to match the names of the relevant Remedy forms: *CTM_People*, *HPD_HelpDesk*, and *WOI_WorkOrder*.[2] Looking at the data, one immediate issue was that the dates were all numbers. A quick search found that these were being stored in Unix or POSIX time, which is the number of seconds since January 1, 1970. This is one of the many things that we can address once we get to Power BI.

---

[2]This approach is not documented. After mentioning it to BMC personnel, I did a webinar for one of their support executives, who was excited about the possibilities and planned to show it to other customers.

Within Power BI, we choose *SQL Server* database as the data source and then enter the *Server, Database,* and credentials.[3] We add a query for each of our desired views.

The only reason we need *CTM_People* is to look up the first and last name of support staff. As explained in a previous footnote, the mechanics of logging in with a Common Access Card (CAC) meant that the *login ID* displayed within Remedy was a bunch of numbers. Remedy forms take care of this for the *assignee* of the ticket but not for the *submitter* of the ticket. We can use this *CTM_People* view to fix that issue. As shown in Figure 84, we set up a relationship between these tables and link the *Submitter* and *Remedy_Login_ID* columns. When it comes time to display who submitted the ticket, we grab the name from *CTM_People* in order to display the actual name.

Figure 84. *Relationships between the CTM_People and HPD_HelpDesk/WOI_Workgroups views*

---

[3]One problem was that Power BI has a limit of 10,000 tables/views. So I could actually select the views I wanted. Instead, just pick any table. Then go into the *Advanced Editor* and put the correct view name in there. Rename the query to match the correct view name.

For both *HPD_HelpDesk* (which contains incidents) and *WOI_WorkOrders* (which contains work orders[4]), we create a custom *SubmitDateUSAFA* column using this formula: `= #datetime(1970, 1, 1, 0, 0, 0) + #duration(0, -6, 0, [Submit_Date])`. This converts from the Unix date discussed previously. The *duration* function takes account of the time zone so that the time is mountain rather than Coordinated Universal Time (UTC), previously known as Greenwich Mean Time. As with previous examples, we create a *DaysPassed* column that shows the number of days since the *SubmitDateUSAFA*: `DaysPassed - DateTime.From(DateTime.LocalNow()) - [SubmitDateUSAFA]`. This is particularly important here as we want to flag (and do special visualizations) for any ticket open longer than our *service level agreement* (such as 7 days). The main other challenge was that the *Status* was stored as a numeric value. We duplicated the *Status* column and then *Replaced Values* with the corresponding text values (Assigned, In Progress, Completed, Resolved, etc.).[5]

One of my current tasks at the Air Force Academy is to manage a particular support team that uses this same system. This often involves submitting tickets to other support teams. It is useful to follow up on these tickets. Figure 85 shows an example of how this approach can be customized. We use the same queries as before but now filter the data to only show tickets submitted by the members of that particular support team. The report then shows exactly who it is assigned to and its current status.

---

[4]In a nutshell, incidents are things that are broken (like being unable to send an email), while work orders are new work (like creating an account).

[5]Since these were not documented, figuring out what each number represented meant looking in the database for the status and then looking that ticket up in the Remedy to see how its status was represented.

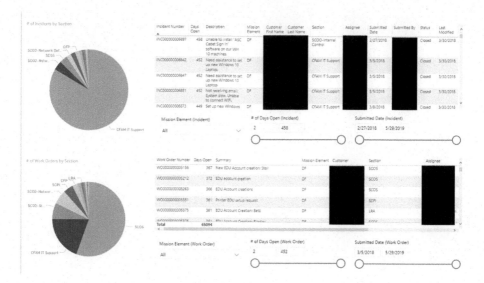

Figure 85. *Power BI dashboard showing the status of tickets submitted by a particular support team*

CHAPTER 14

Displaying and Working with Office Documents

For Office 365 *modern pages*, the SharePoint File Viewer makes it easy to display Office files (Word, Excel, and PowerPoint) as well as other documents within SharePoint.[1] As our first example, we will add two *named parts* from an Excel file to a page, giving the result in Figure 86.

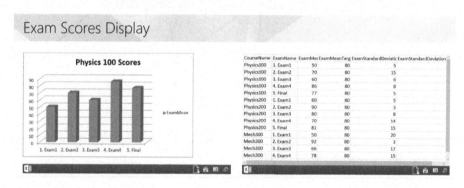

Figure 86. *Two File viewer web parts showing named parts from an Excel file*

---

[1] The *File Viewer* replaces the *Excel Web Access* web part from SharePoint 2013. The other techniques in this chapter can also be accomplished in older versions of SharePoint.

© Jeffrey M. Rhodes 2019
J. M. Rhodes, *Creating Business Applications with Office 365*,
https://doi.org/10.1007/978-1-4842-5331-1_14

To get started, we add the Excel file to a document library. Next, we edit the page, click the plus symbol, and select *File viewer* as shown in Figure 87. We navigate to the Excel file we want to display and then select *Table* or *Chart* for what to display and then type in the *Table Name*. Note that the *named range* in your Excel file works as well.[2] This is shown in Figure 88.

Figure 87. *Adding a File Viewer to a page*

Figure 88. *Configuring the File viewer to display a Table and then a specific Table name*

---

[2]If I just want to display the most relevant part of the Excel file, I will often enter in *Print_Area* for the Table name. This will give the print area defined to be printed out (if that has been set).

Displaying a Word or PowerPoint file is a matter of using the same *File viewer* that we saw in Figure 87. If users need to edit the file, I like to have a dedicated editing page rather than pointing the user to the document library. This forces the user to edit the file in the browser rather than having the choice of using the client Excel, Word, or PowerPoint application. The problem with the client application is that they lock the file, preventing others from editing it at the same time.

Our first task is to get the editing URL. We do that by opening the file in *Excel Online*. Depending on your settings, you can either just click the file or choose the option as shown in Figure 89. That gives us the URL we want:

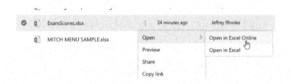

Figure 89.   *Opening the file in Excel Online*

```
https://plattecanyon.sharepoint.com/:x:/r/samples/_layouts/15/
Doc.aspx?sourcedoc=%7Bfa53511f-bfb2-4195-9305-31f0bcfb52fe%7D&a
ction=default&uid=%7BFA53511F-BFB2-4195-9305-31F0BCFB52FE%7D&Li
stItemId=1&ListId=%7B0ABEC394-F3C8-4952-A56F-F771868D49AE%7D&od
sp=1&env=prod
```

Our next step is to generate our embed code. The simplest way is to go to the *File* tab ➤ *Share* ➤ *Embed*. Then grab the embed code as shown in Figure 90.

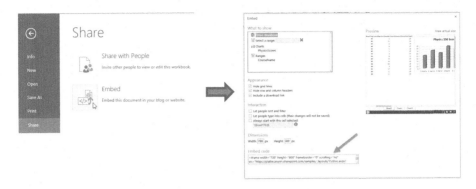

Figure 90. *Generating the Excel embed code*

```
<iframe width="700" height="600" frameborder="0" scrolling="no"
src="https://plattecanyon.sharepoint.com/samples/_layouts/15/
Doc.aspx?sourcedoc={fa53511f-bfb2-4195-9305-31f0bcfb52fe}&actio
n=embedview&wdAllowInteractivity=False&wdHideGridlines=True&wdH
ideHeaders=True&wdDownloadButton=True&wdInConfigurator=True">
</iframe>
```

Notice that the highlighted area is all the *src* of the HTML iFrame. We replace this with the complete URL that we generated previously by editing the Excel document. Here is the result:

```
<iframe width="700" height="600" frameborder="0" scrolling="no"
src="https://plattecanyon.sharepoint.com/:x:/r/samples/_
layouts/15/Doc.aspx?sourcedoc=%7Bfa53511f-bfb2-4195-9305-31f0bc
fb52fe%7D&action=default&uid=%7BFA53511F-BFB2-4195-9305-31F0BCF
B52FE%7D&ListItemId=1&ListId=%7B0ABEC394-F3C8-4952-A56F-F771868
D49AE%7D&odsp=1&env=prod"></iframe>
```

We add an *Embed* web part (Figure 91) and then paste in the updated iFrame code. Figure 92 shows the result. Multiple users can edit the Excel file simultaneously. Note that users without sufficient rights to edit the file, however, will get an error message.

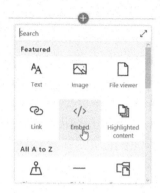

Figure 91. *Adding the Embed web part*

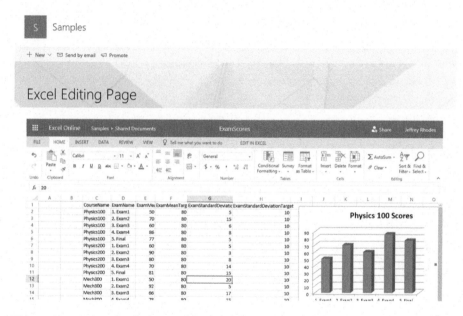

Figure 92. *Excel editing page result*

If we want to get fancier and add our own JavaScript, we need to use a classic page. To do this in Office 365,[3] we go to *Site Contents* ➤ *Site Pages* ➤ *New Wiki Page* as shown in Figure 93. In this example, we have an Excel file with named parts *_Day1* through *_Day31* as shown in Figure 95. The idea is that the staff will upload a new Excel file showing the daily menu (breakfast, lunch, and dinner) for the month. We will then use JavaScript to automatically display the right named part based on the day of the month. Since we are in classic SharePoint, we add the *Excel Web Access* web part as shown in Figure 94. We select the Excel file and enter the *named part* similar to how we described for the preceding *File viewer* . We initially set *_Day1* as the part.

Figure 93. *Adding a classic (Wiki) page*

---

[3]For SharePoint 2013 or older versions, this is how you will do it for all your pages.

Figure 94. *Adding the Excel Web Access web part in a classic/wiki SharePoint page*

We use *Excel Services* to programmatically work with the web part[4] as shown in Listing 16.

Listing 16. JavaScript to programmatically set the named part for the Excel Web Access web part

```
var ewa = null;
var itemCount = 1;

// Add event handler for onload event.
if (window.attachEvent) {
    window.attachEvent("onload", ewaOnPageLoad);
}
else {
    window.addEventListener("DOMContentLoaded", ewaOnPageLoad,
    false);
}
```

---

[4]See https://msdn.microsoft.com/en-us/library/office/ee589016.aspx for more information.

```javascript
// Add event handler for applicationReady event.
function ewaOnPageLoad() {
    Ewa.EwaControl.add_applicationReady(onApplicationReady);
}

function onApplicationReady() {
    // Get a reference to the Excel Services Web Part.
    ewa = Ewa.EwaControl.getInstances().getItem(0);

    // Get a reference to the workbook.
    var wkBook = ewa.getActiveWorkbook();

    // Only run if in Named Item view
    if (wkBook.getIsNamedItemView()) {
        // Get the collection of named items in the workbook.
        var items = wkBook.getNamedItems();
        // build named range based on day of month
        var today = new Date();
        var dayNum = today.getDate();
        var rangeName = "_Day" + dayNum;

        // Get the next named item.
        var item = items.getItemByName(rangeName);

        // Activate the specified named item.
        // Pass in named item as userContext.
        item.activateAsync(activateNamedItemsCallBack, item);
    }
    else {
        // alert("Not in NamedItem view.");
    }
}
```

```
function activateNamedItemsCallBack(asyncResult) {
    // Get named item from userContext.
    //alert("Set named item");
}
```

We start by defining our *ewa* (for Excel Web Access) and *itemcount* global variables. We then "wire up" the *ewaOnPageLoad* function for different browsers so that it is called as soon as the page loads. It in turn calls the *onApplicationReady* function, which is where all the good stuff happens. In there, we set *ewa* to be the first Excel Services web part on the page.[5] We then call the *getActiveWorkbook* method to find the Excel file being displayed in the web part. We then check that it is in "Named Item View," since otherwise the rest of the code is irrelevant. If so, we can programmatically get a list of all the named parts. These are shown from within Excel in Figure 95. Next, we programmatically build the name of the part we want. We figure out *today* and then use the JavaScript *getDate()* method to get the day of the month (22 on the day I am writing this). We then build the *rangeName* variable to be the right named part name (*_Day22* in our example). We then set the *item* variable to be that actual named part object by calling the *getItemByName* method of the collection of named parts. Finally, we call that named part's *activateAsync* method, passing in the name of the function we want to all (*activateNamedItemsCallBack*) and the new named part. We don't need to do anything within this function, but note the commented-out alert box that you could uncomment for testing. Figure 96 shows the result for the December menu. Notice that circled *DEC 22* date.

---

[5]If you had multiple Excel Web Access parts on the page, you would need to do logic here rather than just using the first one (*getItems(0)*).

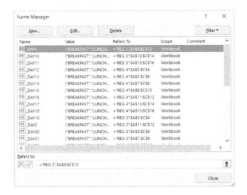

Figure 95. *Named parts in Excel file*

X▉ Mitchell Hall Daily Menu

BREAKFAST	LUNCH	DINNER
ASSORTED CEREAL/ OATMEAL & GRITS SAUSAGE LINKS HARD BOILED EGGS SCRAMBLED EGGS W/ HAM & CHEESE COUNTRY HASH BROWN POTATOES CHILLED ORANGE JUICE MILK/ SOY MILK COFFEE/ HOT CHOCOLATE/ ICE WATER FRESH FRUIT/ FRUIT YOGURT *INDIVIDUAL PISTACHIOS *GREEN MACHINE NAKED JUICE *FRESH HONEYDEW FRUIT TUB	THURSDAY DEC 22 HAMBURGER PASTA VEGETARIAN VEGETABLES W/ CHICKPEAS & COUSCOUS (V) FRESH SPINACH SALAD/ ASSORTED SALAD DRESSING *WHOLE WHEAT ROLLS BUTTER/ MARGARINE CHILLED PEACH ORCHARD PUNCH MILK/ SOY MILK/ COFFEE/ ICE WATER FRESH FRUIT *SNICKERDOODLE COOKIE *FRESH RED GRAPES FRUIT TUB	ZESTY ROAST BEEF POTATO CRUSTED COD/ INDIVIDUAL TARTAR SAUCE VEGETARIAN POTATO CASSEROLE (V) GARLIC ROASTED MASHED POTATOES/ BROWN GRAVY CHATEAU BLEND VEGETABLES FRESH SALAD BAR/ ASSORTED SALAD DRESSING *ASSORTED GLACIER ROLLS BUTTER/ MARGARINE CHILLED LEMONADE/ BERRY RAIN GATORADE *CHOCOLATE MILK MILK/ SOY MILK/ COFFEE/ ICE WATER FRESH FRUIT/ FROZEN SOFT SERVE DIRT PUDDING

Figure 96. *Resulting menu page showing the _Day22 named part set programmatically*

CHAPTER 15

Building a Help Ticketing System in PowerApps and SharePoint: New Ticket Form

Our help desk at the Academy did not have a good system for either walk-in traffic in particular. We introduced the SharePoint list data source for a new solution back in Figure 7. All our users did not have Office 365 accounts, but that wasn't a problem because the "kiosk" computer would be signed in. Figure 96 shows our initial look at the *New Ticket* form.

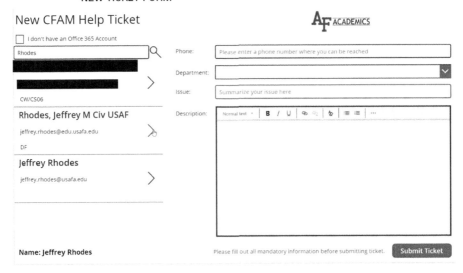

Figure 97. *New Ticket form showing the lookup of users in Office 365 as well as cues for proper entry*

For this form, we choose to create a *Canvas app from blank* and choose the *Tablet* format.[1] Our next task is to add a *SharePoint* data source and point it to our *Help Tickets* list. We also add an *Office365Users* data source that we will use to look up users (for those who have Office 365 accounts). Finally, we add an *Office365* Outlook data source for sending email. These data connections are shown in Figure 98.

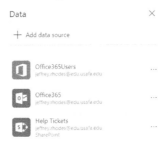

Figure 98. *SharePoint, Users, and Outlook data sources*

---

[1] I chose *Tablet* in this case since it was primarily intended to run on a kiosk computer in our help desk. We will see that the technician form in the next chapter uses the *Phone* format.

Our first big task is to allow the user to find himself or herself in Office 365. We add a *Text Input* for the search and an icon for the magnifying glass. We use a *Gallery* control to display the results so that users can type in their last name and find their record. To make that work, we set its *Items* property to

```
Office365Users.SearchUser({searchTerm:searchUser.Text, top: 10})
```

This is a good introduction to PowerApps programming. I like how its web-based editor uses a single interface for both setting properties and programming. In traditional editors like *Visual Studio* and languages like C#, you set properties in one window and then put the programming into a separate "code behind" file. In PowerApps, we can add programming right into the same place where we set the property values.[2] In the preceding code, we set the *Items* property of the control by calling the *SearchUser* method of the *Office365Users* data connection. We set the *searchTerm* parameter to be the *Text* property of our *searchUser* Text Input control. We limit our values to the top 10.

We set the *Gallery* to be a *Title* layout and associate the controls with the *DisplayName, Mail,* and *Department* attributes from Office 365. To make it easier to tell which user we have selected, we put this logic in the *Fill* property of the DisplayName label:

```
If(ThisItem.IsSelected, Color.Yellow, RGBA(0, 0, 0, 0))
```

This means that if the *IsSelected* property of that record is true, then the background fill color is yellow. Otherwise, it is black.

Similarly, we set the *Text* property of the *UserName* label at the bottom left of Figure 97 to be

---

[2]As we have discussed, programming is largely a matter of reading/setting properties, responding to events, and calling methods. Events are listed right along with properties in the editor, making it as easy to handle them as it is to set properties.

```
"Name: " & If(NoO365Account.Value,FirstNameInput.Text & " "
& LastNameInput.Text,If(UsersGallery.Visible, UsersGallery.
Selected.GivenName & " " & UsersGallery.Selected.Surname, ""))
```

This code makes more sense if we refer to Figure 99, which shows the form when the user checks the *I don't have an Office 365 Account* box. When that box is true, we concatenate the first name and last name that the user enters. If not, we see if the *UsersGallery* is visible (we hide it until the user starts searching since it otherwise defaults to the first user) and, if so, concatenate the *GivenName* and *Surname* properties. Otherwise, we leave the name part blank. Here is the code for the *UsersGallery Visible* property:

```
(!NoO365Account.Value && (searchUser.Text <> "" &&
!IsBlank(searchUser.Text)))
```

Figure 99. *Entering name and email when no Office 365 account*

In words, this says to show the Gallery when the *I don't have an Office 365 Account* box is unchecked AND when search text is both not an empty string and not blank.

Note how there is a label showing that the email format is invalid. We make this work by setting its *Visible* value to be

```
If(NoO365Account.Value,If(IsMatch(EmailInput.Text,Match.Email)
|| IsBlank(EmailInput.Text), false, true), false)
```

This demonstrates a "nested" If condition. If the *NoO365Account* box is checked, then we see if we have a valid email format (the second If). If not, the *Visible* is false. To check the valid format, we use the *IsMatch* method, passing it what the user entered and telling it to match it to an Email format. Since email is not required, we also allow it to be blank. In those cases, *Visible* is false. Otherwise (not blank and invalid), it is true. We use similar logic to set the *BorderColor* to maroon[3] when the format is invalid:

```
If(NoO365Account.Value,If(IsMatch(EmailInput.Text,Match.Email)
|| IsBlank(EmailInput.Text), RGBA(0, 18, 107, 1), RGBA(184, 0,
0, 1)), RGBA(0, 18, 107, 1))
```

Let's look at the right side of Figure 97. We set the *HintText* property for the Phone and Issue to give users more information on what to enter. For Department, we could have linked it to the choices within SharePoint (see the next chapter for an example), but we don't want there to be a default that the user just accepts, so we set the values explicitly with the initial choice being blank. We then make sure there is a selection before allowing the form to be submitted. To do this, we set the *Items* property to be

```
["","DF","DFAN","DFAS","DFB","DFBL","DFC","DFCE","DFCS","DFEC",
"DFEG","DFEI","DFEM","DFENG","DFF","DFH","DFK","DFL","DFLIB",
"DFM","DFMI","DFMS","DFP","DFPS","DFPY","DFR","DFRO",
"DFRO (UAS)","DFS","Other"]
```

Issue is the single-most important field, so we give it a maroon highlight until the user enters information. We do that by setting the *BorderColor* property to be

```
If(IssueInput.Text = "", RGBA(184, 0, 0, 1), RGBA(0, 18, 107, 1))
```

---

[3]RGBA stands for red green blue alpha, where each value goes from 0 to 255. Alpha gives the amount of transparency. A tool like Photoshop is good from coming up with these values. Note as in other examples that you can also use named colors like *Color.Yellow*.

The last task before we write the ticket data to SharePoint is to ensure that we have all the required information. For that, we make the *RequiredValuesLabel* and give it the text of "Please fill out mandatory data before submitting the ticket." We set its *Visible* property to be

```
If((DepartmentDropDown.SelectedText.Value = Blank() ||
DepartmentDropDown.SelectedText.Value = "" || IssueInput.Text =
"" || InvalidFormatLabel.Visible), true, false)
```

The || represents an OR condition. So if there is no department selected, no issue entered, or if there is an invalid email format (see the preceding discussion), we show this label.

We are now ready to write the ticket back to our SharePoint data source.[4] We handle the *OnSelect* event as shown in Figure 100. Notice how you can drag down the entry space in the browser to give more space for typing.

Figure 100. *Handling the OnSelect event and writing ticket data to the SharePoint data source*

Listing 17 shows the code after clicking the *Format text* link shown in Figure 100. We will go through each section in turn.

---

[4]Note that this would work for an Excel or other data source as well.

Listing 17. OnSelect code for writing ticket information to a
SharePoint list

```
If(
    RequiredValuesLabel.Visible,
    false,
    If(
        NoO365Account.Value,
        Patch(
            'Help Tickets',
            Defaults('Help Tickets'),
            {
                Issue: IssueInput.Text,
                'Phone Number': PhoneInput.Text,
                Department: DepartmentDropDown.SelectedText,
                Description: DescriptionInput.HtmlText,
                'User (Not Office 365)': LastNameInput.Text &
                ", " & FirstNameInput.Text,
                'Email (Not Office 365)': EmailInput.Text
            }
        ),
        Patch(
            'Help Tickets',
            Defaults('Help Tickets'),
            {
                Issue: IssueInput.Text,
                'Phone Number': PhoneInput.Text,
                Department: DepartmentDropDown.SelectedText,
                Description: DescriptionInput.HtmlText,
```

```
                'User (Office 365)': {
                    '@odata.type': "#Microsoft.Azure.
                    Connectors.SharePoint.SPListExpandedUser",
                    ODataType: Blank(),
                    Claims: Concatenate(
                        "i:0#.f|membership|",
                        UsersGallery.Selected.Mail
                    ),
                    DisplayName: UsersGallery.Selected.
                    DisplayName,
                    Email: UsersGallery.Selected.Mail,
                    Department: "",
                    JobTitle: "",
                    Picture: ""
                }
            }
        )
    )
);
If(
    !RequiredValuesLabel.Visible,
    Office365.SendEmail(
        "df_cfam@usafa.edu",
        "New Ticket - " & IssueInput.Text & " (" & UserName.
        Text & ")",
        "User: " & UserName.Text & "<br/><br/>Issue: "
        & IssueInput.Text & "<br/><br/>Description: " &
        DescriptionInput.HtmlText,
        {
            IsHtml: true,
            Importance: Normal
        }
```

```
);
Reset(IssueInput);
Reset(DescriptionInput);
Reset(DepartmentDropDown);
Reset(EmailInput);
Reset(LastNameInput);
Reset(FirstNameInput);
Reset(searchUser);
Reset(NoO365Account);
Reset(PhoneInput);
Reset(UsersGallery);
UpdateContext({popupVisible: true}),
false
)
```

We first check to see if our *RequiredValuesLabel* is visible. If so, we
know we have an error (and don't have to repeat all our earlier error-
checking logic) and return *false*. Next, we check to see if the user has an
Office 365 account. If so, we send the *User (Office 365)* info. Otherwise, we
send the *User (Not Office 365)* information. Note that we added the non-
365 email as a separate SharePoint column so that we could use that to
send an email when the technician resolves the ticket. To actually write the
information to SharePoint, we call the *Patch* method. The first parameter is
the data source (*Help Tickets* list). The second parameter is the *BaseRecord*
we want to modify. We call the *Defaults* method to create a record. This
also puts any default values into the columns. For example, the *Status*
defaults to *New* and we don't have to write it here. Finally, we pass in an
object (defined with {}) with properties corresponding to the column name
in the SharePoint list. Note how column names with spaces need to be in
single quotes. The "no Office 365" case is simpler because we just pass in

the first name, last name, and email. When we have a 365 user, however, we need to pass in an object. Here it is again:

```
{
    '@odata.type': "#Microsoft.Azure.Connectors.SharePoint.
    SPListExpandedUser",
    ODataType: Blank(),
    Claims: Concatenate(
        "i:0#.f|membership|",
        UsersGallery.Selected.Mail
    ),
    DisplayName: UsersGallery.Selected.DisplayName,
    Email: UsersGallery.Selected.Mail,
    Department: "",
    JobTitle: "",
    Picture: ""
}
```

We start with an OData (Open Data Protocol) type to tell PowerApps that this is a SharePoint person. We take advantage of the fact that the *Claims* (credentials) are in the format i:0#.f|membership|jeffrey.rhodes@ edu.usafa.edu. We need that, the *DisplayName* and the *Email,* in order to represent the proper user to SharePoint. From there we use the *Office365* (Outlook) data connection and call its *SendEmail* function, passing in the address, the subject (note how we put the issue and the user in there), and the body (showing the user, issue, and description). Notice how to use the HTML break (<br />) tag to put in hard returns. That goes along with setting the *IsHtml* property to true. PowerApps defaults to a low importance email, so we set it to *Normal.* From there, we now want to *Reset* all the entries so that this kiosk form is ready for the next user. Notice how we can separate commands with semicolons (;). That's it, except for the *UpdateContext* line, which we will cover next.

In first testing this form, users weren't sure if their ticket got submitted correctly. So I decided to add a popup confirmation. For that, we use a local variable that we will call *popupVisible*. It defaults to false, but we use the *UpdateContext* command to set it to true. Figure 101 shows how we implement this as a group of a button, icon (the X at the upper right), and a label. We set the *Visible* property of the group to be *popupVisible*. Clicking either the button or the X sets the *popupVisible* variable back to false, which closes the popup and makes the form ready for the next user.

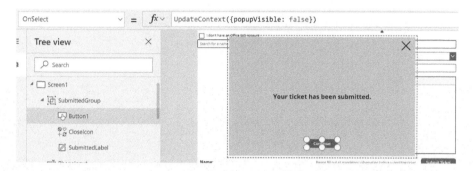

Figure 101. *Popup confirmation group with its Visible property controlled by the popupVisible local variable*

CHAPTER 16

Continuing the Help Ticketing System: Technician Form

Now that we have our tickets in the SharePoint list, we can significantly improve the productivity of our help desk technicians by letting them manage tickets on their mobile devices (as well as their computer if desired). We will let PowerApps build the basic plumbing of the form and then customize from there.

In PowerApps, we choose to *Start from data*, which defaults to a Canvas app with a Phone layout. We then tell it to use our SharePoint list as the data source. PowerApps makes us three screens: *Browse, Detail,* and *Edit*. We will go through the edits to each of these screens in turn.

On the *Browse* screen, we want to add a *Status* drop-down box so that technician can filter the tickets by status. We default it to *New* so that new tickets will show up by default. We also want to change the Search from the default of searching by Title (*Issue* in our case) to search by Technician. Finally, we want to edit what information is displayed in *BrowseGallery1*. All of these are shown in Figure 102.

© Jeffrey M. Rhodes 2019
J. M. Rhodes, *Creating Business Applications with Office 365*,
https://doi.org/10.1007/978-1-4842-5331-1_16

Figure 102. *The Browse screen in our Help Technician application*

We insert a label and drop-down box for our status. We move the gallery down a bit to make room. We set the *Items* property of the drop-down box to be `Choices('Help Tickets'.Status)`. This ties it to the *Choice* column in SharePoint and makes sure the choices on the form are updated when the SharePoint column is edited. For the *Search* functionality, we change the *HintText* to give an indication that the search is for the assigned technician. The next step is to change the *Items* property for the gallery to be

```
SortByColumns(Filter('Help Tickets', Status.Value=TicketStatusBox.
Selected.Value, IsBlank('Assigned Technician') ||
StartsWith('Assigned Technician'.Value, TextSearchBox1.Text)),
"Created", If(SortDescending1, Descending, Ascending))
```

We take advantage of the fact that the *Filter* method can take multiple parameters. So in addition to the default *StartsWith* parameter, which we adjust by making it applicable to the *Assigned Technician* column,[1] we add

---

[1]Notice how we use an *OR* condition (||) and *IsBlank()* to account for the fact that there won't be a technician assigned at first. Without this, only tickets with an assigned technician were displayed (and we couldn't then see the tickets to assign someone).

the matching of the *Status* to what we select in the *Status* drop-down box. The last parameter sets the order of searching. The *SortDescending1* is a context variable that is toggled by the up and down arrows at the top of the screen. Its *OnSelect* event has this value: `UpdateContext({SortDescending1: !SortDescending1})`. This means to make *SortDescending1* true if it was false and vice versa. We list *Descending* first since *SortDescending1* defaults to false, and we want an *Ascending* sort initially so that the oldest tickets are at the top.

One complication that took me hours to debug[2] later is that the minute we use the *Filter* command on a "complex" column like *Status* (since it is a SharePoint choice column), PowerApps limits us to 500 records by default. This is a big problem since our newest tickets are at the end of the SharePoint list. You can raise this limit but that can affect performance. To be fair, the PowerApps editor warned me about the filter limit; I just ignored it:). You can see the warning icon in Figure 102. Fixing this turned out to be non-trivial. I made *Single Line Text* columns called *Ticket Status* and *Ticket Assigned Technician* and used a workflow[3] to automatically update these columns when either the *Status* or *Assigned Technician* values changed. The updated *Items* value then looks like this:

```
SortByColumns(Filter('Help Tickets', 'Ticket
Status'=TicketStatusBox.Selected.Value, 'Ticket Assigned
Technician'="" || StartsWith('Ticket Assigned Technician',
TextSearchBox1.Text)), "Created", If(SortDescending1,
Descending, Ascending))
```

---

[2]I was making other edits to the form and couldn't get any of the new tickets I created for testing to show up. I eventually figured out that only the first 500 records were showing up (e.g., all our resolved and currently being worked tickets).

[3]A SharePoint 2013 workflow worked better than *Flow* in this case as *Flow* wanted to update all the columns (particularly the mandatory ones).

Notice how we needed to get rid of the *IsBlank()* function as well. The good news is these changes fixed the issue.

Our last task on this screen is to edit the information shown in the gallery control. Referring again to Figure 102, we add two extra labels to the card so that we can show the Issue, User, Status, Assigned Technician, and Number of Days Open. Since it is not obvious what the data represents, we add a description before the value as in "Status: " & ThisItem.Status. Value. As you might recall, we can have either an Office 365 user or a non-Office 365 user. To avoid having to confuse our screen with two values (one of which would be blank), we use this logic for our user display:

```
If(IsBlank(ThisItem.'User (Office 365)'.DisplayName),
ThisItem.'User (Not Office 365)', ThisItem.'User (Office 365)'.
DisplayName)
```

The Number of Days functionality takes advantage of the useful *DateDiff* function to give us the number of days between two dates:

```
"Number of Days Open: " & If(Status.Value = "Resolved",DateDiff
(Created,'Resolved Date'),DateDiff(Created,Now()))
```

If the ticket has been resolved, we stop the clock and use the difference between *Resolved Date* and *Created*. Otherwise, we use the *Now()* function to get the difference between the current date and time and *Created*.

On the Details screen (Figure 103), we click *Edit fields* to display the desired data and to add or delete fields (columns). We display the *ID* primary key value from SharePoint but rename it as the *Ticket Number*. We also show the *Created* date so that the technician can see when the ticket was first entered. The *(custom)* identifier means that we have unlocked the data card to change the controls and/or the formulas. We did that for the user to put in the same formula described previously. The renaming of ID is a customization as was including our *Number of Days Open* information below the *Created* value. We also unlocked Description and Notes to use an *HTML Text* control so that the HTML/Rich Text that we input in the form in the last chapter as well as the notes that the technicians add will be displayed correctly.[4]

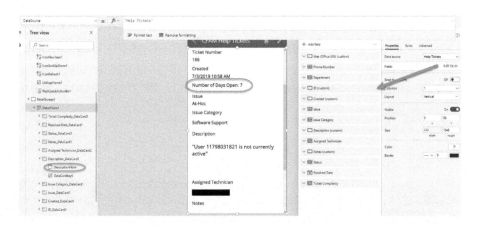

Figure 103. *The Details screen in our Help Technician application*

The *Edit* form (also used for new records) is similar to the one for users discussed in the last chapter. However, we need to include all the fields rather than just the ones to open a ticket. This is because a technician may use this form to open and close a ticket all in one action, for example, when they help a customer over the phone and then document the ticket afterward. Figure 104 shows the form in the development environment. As with other screens, we use *Edit fields* to add or delete what fields/columns we want to include. Many of these are customized. The biggest reason is because PowerApps uses combo boxes rather than drop-down boxes for choices like Department, Issue Category, Assigned Technician, and Status. Changing

---

[4]We could have used the *Rich text editor* control as well and in fact that works better when it comes time to edit the *Description*.

this[5] involves unlocking the data card, adding a *Drop down* control and making it the same size and position as the combo box, changing its *Items* property (to something like `Choices('Help Tickets'.Status)`), and then deleting the combo box. This results in a couple of error messages. You click the messages and substitute the name of your drop-down box for the old combo box name. The most important is for the *Update* method of the data card. For example, for *Status* you change it to `StatusDropDown.Selected`. The other main challenge was that the drop-down boxes did not correctly display the current value when you edited an item. That was because the *Default* value needed to be set to an expression like `ThisItem.Status.Value`.

Figure 104. *The New/Edit screen in our Help Technician application*

The other main change was to enable the entry of HTML/Rich Text into the *Description*. This may be fixed in future PowerApps releases, but using the *HTML Text* control would not allow the technician to enter information. Switching to the *Rich text editor* control worked fine, however.

---

[5]I didn't notice the problem with the default combo box control when testing on a computer. However, when I published a version to the help desk and a technician tested on his iPad, each combo box displayed the iPad's virtual keyboard and that got in the way of filling in the form. Switching to drop-down boxes fixed that problem.

A time-saving feature is to set the *Resolved Date* value to the current date when the technician changes the *Status* to Resolved. To do that, we unlock the Resolved Date Data Card and set the *DefaultDate* to `If(StatusDropDown.Selected.Value = "Resolved", Today(), Parent.Default)`. We check the value of the *StatusDropDown* and, if it is Resolved, we set it to the built-in *Today()* function. Otherwise, we use the original value, which is the *Parent.Default*.

A disconcerting problem surfaced when using the application to change a ticket status. Since we are filtering on status (see Figure 102), this meant that our ticket disappeared once we saved it. For example, we open the application, change the *Status* filter to *Assigned/In Progress,* and select the ticket that we want, which takes us to the *Details* screen. We edit the ticket and change its status to *Resolved*. We are returned to the *Details* screen, but now a different ticket is displayed. That's because our current item doesn't meet the filter. To fix that, the most logical solution (to me at least) was to change the filter to our new status (*Resolved* in this example). To make this work, we need to know our current filter value and, if the new status is different, change the filter.

Another related requirement is to send the user an email when the ticket is resolved. For that logic, we need to know our current ticket status and then send the email if the status has changed to *Resolved*.[6] For both of these requirements, we need to share values between different screens and thus need global variables. We set them when we create a new ticket (*OnSelect* event for the *IconNewItem1* button):

```
Set(CurrentFilterStatus, TicketStatusBox.Selected.Value);
Set(CurrentTicketStatus, "New");
NewForm(EditForm1);Navigate(EditScreen1, ScreenTransition.None)
```

---

[6]We don't just want to send an email whenever the status is *Resolved* since the user could get duplicate emails such as in the situation where a technician edits a ticket to add additional notes. Instead, we only want to send the email the one time the status is changed to *Resolved*.

Notice the syntax for setting a global variable: *Set(<variable name>: <variable value>)*. As we have seen before, we separate statements with semicolons. The *NewForm* and *Navigate* methods were already in place from the wizard that built the form. We have similar logic when we edit an item:

```
Set(CurrentFilterStatus, TicketStatusBox.Selected.Value);
Set(CurrentTicketStatus, DataCardValue7.Selected.Value );
EditForm(EditForm1);Navigate(EditScreen1, ScreenTransition.None)
```

We read the *DataCardValue7* to get the current status of the ticket in this case.

Now that we have what we need to determine if the status is different from the current filter, we need to allow our status filter to be set programmatically (instead of just by the user selecting an option). We need another global variable (since *TicketStatusBox* is on a different screen. We set its *Default* value to this variable, which we will name *ticketStatusDefault*. We don't need to initialize it, since when it is blank the value will use the first one in the list, which is the *New* value we want.

We take care of both these requirements (updating the filter and sending a resolution email) by handling the *OnSuccess* event[7] for the form. This is shown in Listing 18:

Listing 18. OnSuccess code for updating the filter and sending a resolution email

```
If(
    CurrentFilterStatus<>StatusDropDown.Selected.Value,
    Set(
        ticketStatusDefault,
        StatusDropDown.Selected.Value
    ),
```

---

[7]We could do this in the *OnSelect* event for the save button (*IconAccept1* control), but we then have a problem if there is an error. The filter would have changed and now our form would potentially disappear. Instead, we wait until we know our changes were successful.

```
     false)
If(

    (StatusDropDown.Selected.Value = "Resolved" &&
    CurrentTicketStatus <> "Resolved"),
    Office365.SendEmail(
        If(
            IsBlank('User (Office 365)_DataCard1'.Default),
            DataCardValue16.Text,
            Substitute(
                First(DataCardValue10.SelectedItems).Email,
                "@edu.usafa.edu",
                "@usafa.edu"
            )
        ),
        "Your Ticket Has Been Resolved - " & DataCardValue9.Text,
        "Dear " & If(
            IsBlank('User (Office 365)_DataCard1'.Default),
            DataCardValue11.Text,
            First(DataCardValue10.SelectedItems).DisplayName
        ) & "<br /><br />We are pleased to inform you that
        your ticket has been resolved. Here are the details:
        <br /><br />Issue: " & DataCardValue9.Text & "<br
        /><br />Description: " & DescriptionRichText.
        HtmlText & "<br /><br />Assigned Technician: " &
        AssignedTechnicianDropDown.Selected.Value & "<br /><br
        />Notes: " & NotesRichText.HtmlText & "<br /><br />If
        you have any questions or would like to address this or
        another issue, please call us at 555-1212 or email us
        at <a href='mailTo:emailhidden@usafa.edu'> emailhidden@
        usafa.edu</a>. <br /><br /><b><a href='https://forms.
        office.com/Pages/ResponsePage.aspx?id=Bgq4einwwEWEOX2t
        Gc48Ya2H6jjrY7pBhCORGrOFp91UQzdBMEUyVVk3SzZRQkhVUUVCT
```

```
        1AxSEdFQi4u'>Please take our survey</a></b>.<br /><br
        /><br />Thanks, <br /><br />The CFAM Help Desk",
        {
            IsHtml: true,
            Importance: Normal
        }
    ),
    false
);
;Back()
```

We compare our *CurrentFilterStatus* global variable to what we just set on the edit form (*StatusDropDown.Selected.Value*). If those are different, we set the *ticketStatusDefault* variable to be the new status. This is enough to change the filter.

We then compare the status from the form to our *CurrentTicketStatus* global variable. If the status just changed to *Resolved*, then we send the user an email. We do some logic to figure out whether they have an Office 365 account or whether to use the email they entered (*DataCardValue16* represents that value on the Edit form). If they have an Office 365 account, we need to take account of the fact that the combo box holding the user information *could* have multiple items selected. So we use the syntax *First(DataCardValue10*.SelectedItems) to get our hands on the user. We then read the *.Email* property. In our implementation at the Air Force Academy, the Office 365 email address is not primary. So we use the *Substitute* method to replace *@edu.usafa.edu* with *@usafa.edu*. The next parameter is the subject. We append the Issue (*DataCardValue*.Text) to it. From there, we define the body of the email. We include the Issue, Description, Assigned Technician, and Notes. Since we are sending an HTML email, we use breaks (<br />) for hard returns and read the

HtmlText property for the Description and Notes. We use the *mailTo:* syntax to allow the user to send a follow-on email and also include a link to a survey (see Figure 61 for an example). Here is how the email looks:

> *To: <User Email>*
>
> *Subject: Your Ticket Has Been Resolved - <Issue>*
>
> *Dear <User Display Name>*
>
> *We are pleased to inform you that your ticket has been resolved. Here are the details:*
>
> *Issue: <Issue>*
>
> *Description: <Description>*
>
> *Assigned Technician: <Technician>*
>
> *Notes: <Notes>*
>
> *If you have any questions or would like to address this or another issue,*
>
> *please call us at <phone number> or email us at <email address>.*
>
> *Please take our survey (hyperlink)*
>
> *Thanks,*
>
> *The CFAM Help Desk*

Finally, we call the original *Back* method to get to the *Details* or *Browse* screen as appropriate.

It didn't take long after releasing this new help ticket solution for users to ask to view their own tickets. We needed to limit it to those

155

users who have an Office 365 account,[8] but it took very little time to edit the application described in this chapter and rename it to *CFAM_ MyHelpTickets*. Figure 105 shows the result.

Figure 105. *The My Help Tickets application*

The user label has a simple formula for its *Text* property:

```
"User: " & User().FullName
```

Rather than a drop-down box showing the different *Status* values, we default to only open tickets but give the option to *Show Resolved Tickets* as well. The *Items* property for the *BrowseGallery1* is a bit different than what we saw earlier:

```
SortByColumns(Filter('Help Tickets', 'User (Office 365)'.
Email = User().Email, If(ShowResolvedTicketsBox.Value, Status.
Value <> "",Status.Value <> "Resolved"), IsBlank(Issue)
|| StartsWith(Issue, TextSearchBox1.Text)), "Created",
If(SortDescending1, Descending, Ascending))
```

---

[8]We will limit to Office 365 users since otherwise we don't have a way to prevent one person from looking up someone else's tickets. Plus, there is no way to launch a PowerApps application unless you have an Office 365 account and it is shared with you. We got by that with our kiosk application for creating a ticket, but there would be security problems with a kiosk to view tickets.

We limit our tickets to the current user by making sure the *Email* property of our SharePoint person column matches the email of the current user. If the *Show Resolved Tickets* box is checked, we take any ticket (make sure the status is not ""). Otherwise, we take all except those with a *Resolved* status.

As you might have guessed from the warning symbol in Figure 105, this initial implementation also suffered from the 500-record limit. Since there were multiple issues here, we fix it a different way. We first set two variables in the *OnStart* event for the application:

```
Set(currentEmail, User().Email); ClearCollect(col, Filter('Help
Tickets', 'User (Office 365)'.Email = currentEmail))
```

The first part makes the *currentEmail* variable and sets it to the current user's email. We need this because putting the *User().Email* value into either the *ClearCollect* function or the *Items* value of gallery causes the delegation error and limits us to 500 records. The *ClearCollect* function makes a collection variable (*col*) from the second parameter, which is the *Filter* of all help tickets with the user's email address.[9] We can then use *col* in our *Items* property for *BrowseGallery1*:

```
SortByColumns(Filter(col, If(ShowResolvedTicketsBox.Value,
Status.Value <> "",Status.Value <> "Resolved"), IsBlank(Issue)
|| StartsWith(Issue, TextSearchBox1.Text)), "Created",
If(SortDescending1, Descending, Ascending))
```

We filter on *col* and don't need to limit to the user's email address since we already took care of that.

For the rest of the application, we delete the Edit screen, hide the "edit" and "new" buttons, and fix the errors (e.g., code that references the missing screen).

---

[9]Note that this solution will run into problems if the user ever exceeds 500 tickets. But that is much better than a limit of 500 tickets total.

CHAPTER 17

Using Power BI for the Help Ticketing System

Our help ticketing solution would not be complete without a Power BI
solution to monitor our tickets. Our SharePoint list is an easy-to-use data
source. Figure 106 shows the results a couple of weeks after going live with
this solution.[1]

---

[1]This was in the summer when many of the faculty were away. The system still
logged about 100 tickets per week.

© Jeffrey M. Rhodes 2019
J. M. Rhodes, *Creating Business Applications with Office 365*,
https://doi.org/10.1007/978-1-4842-5331-1_17

Figure 106. *Power BI visualization of tickets within the last 30 days*

As with earlier Power BI solutions, much of the work is in editing the query. Our first challenge is to get the display name of the *User (Office 365)* People column. As shown in Figure 107, we expand the *FieldValuesAsText* and select that column. We rename that column to *Office 365 User*. We then create a conditional *User* column that will have this *Office 365 User* value if it has a value and otherwise contain *User (Not Office 365)*. See Figure 108.

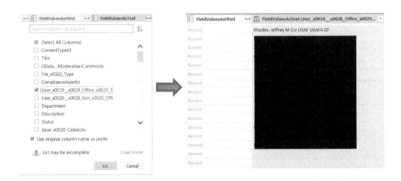

Figure 107. *Expanding FieldValuesAsText to get the DisplayName for the User (Office 365) People column*

160

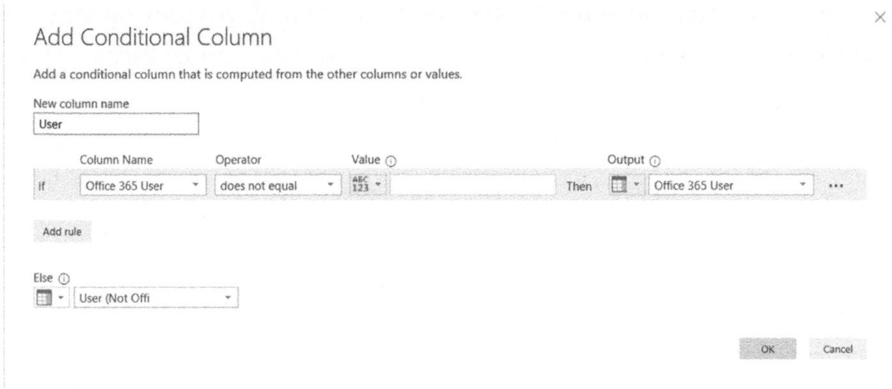

Figure 108. *Conditional column that takes the proper value depending on whether the user had an Office 365 account*

As in previous examples, we want a *Days Open* column. But we want to be a bit more sophisticated in that we will stop counting once the ticket is resolved. That gives us this logic:

```
Days Open =
if [Status] = "Resolved" then
    if ([Resolved Date] > [Created]) then
        [Resolved Date] - [Created]
    else
        0
else
    DateTime.From(DateTime.LocalNow()) - [Created]
```

If the status is *Resolved*, then we make sure that the *Resolved Date* is greater than the *Created* date. If so, the value is the difference. If not, we give it a value of 0.[2] If the ticket has not yet been resolved, we take the

---

[2]We need this extra logic because *Resolved Date* is just a date value without a time. This ends up being the same as 00:00 (midnight). So if a ticket is opened and closed the same day, the *Days Open* ends up being negative. That doesn't make sense, so we use 0 instead.

current date and time and subtract *Created* from that. We then change this type to be a whole number. We use this value in the *Open Tickets > 7 Days* page as well as displaying as a Tooltip on all graphs.

In a similar vein, we make a *Days Since Created* column using this logic:

```
DateTime.From(DateTime.LocalNow()) - [Created]
```

This allows us to see all tickets created during a time period. As you might guess, this is what we use for the *Tickets Last 30 Days* and *Tickets Last 90 Days* pages in Figure 106.

Our last main change[3] is to rename *Id* to *Ticket #*. This keeps us from having to rename it for each visualization.

Much of the work for the visualization is in the *page level filters*. As we see in Figure 109, we limit the *Open Tickets* page to tickets where the *Status* is not *Resolved*. For the *Open Tickets > 7 Days* page, however, we need two filters: *Days Open > 7* and *Status* is not *Resolved*. Since Power BI only allows a single *page level filter*, we put the second filter on every visualization/table on this page. Figure 110 shows an example. For the *Tickets Last 30 Days* page, we can go back to one filter: *Days Since Created* <= 30. We want to include resolved tickets in this case as we want to see the entire workload.

---

[3]The *Description* and *Notes* columns have XML format. However, the approach to replace *null* values with *<div></div>* and then *Parse – XML* did not pay as many dividends here. This may have been due to using the *RichText* controls as in Figure 104.

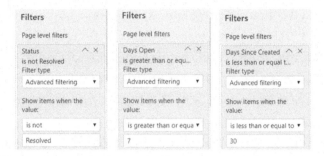

Figure 109. *Page level filters for the Open Tickets, Open Tickets > 7 Days, and Tickets Last 30 Days pages*

Figure 110. *Additional Visual-level filter for the Open Tickets > 7 Days page*

As in past examples, our pie charts have the data we are tracking (*Status* or *Assigned Technician*) as the Legend. We then have the Count of the ID/Ticket # as the *Values*. We rename this to *# of Tickets* to make the labels more understandable. We show *Average of Days Open* as the Tooltips.

The stacked column chart (Figure 111) gives us additional information. We show the *Assigned Technician* along the horizontal axis. The Legend is the *Status*. These are each in a different color. The Value is once again the *Count of ID/Ticket #* that we rename to *# of Tickets*. We display *Average of Days Open* as the Tooltip. As you can see in Figure 111, all of these values show up as the tooltip when we move our mouse over one of the segments of the bar chart. It also shows the *Table* control showing the detailed information.

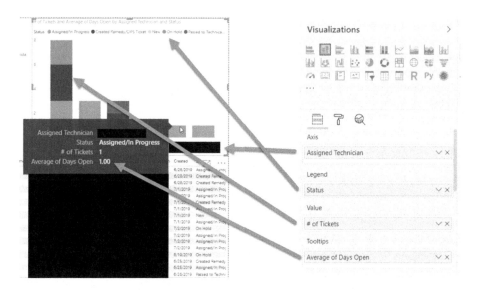

Figure 111. *Stacked column chart showing Axis (Assigned Technician), Legend (Status), Value (Count of Ticket #), and Tooltips (Average of Days Open)*

CHAPTER 18

Leveraging an iFrame to Display Another SharePoint Page

What if we want to display SharePoint content in another page? For example, we might want to show (and interact with) our color calendar (Figure 36). If we are on the same site, then we can add the calendar as a web part (and in this case add the two *Content Editor* web parts holding the legend and calendar code). But if we are in a different site, that is not possible. Our next choice is to *Embed* a page (modern page) or use the *Page Viewer* web part (classic page). Figure 112 shows the result.

© Jeffrey M. Rhodes 2019
J. M. Rhodes, *Creating Business Applications with Office 365*,
https://doi.org/10.1007/978-1-4842-5331-1_18

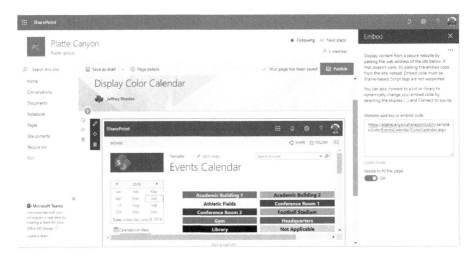

Figure 112. *Embedding one SharePoint page in another page*

The issue is immediately evident. We can tell that this is an embedded page since all the menus and items at the top and left of the page are visible. What we actually want is just the legend and the calendar itself. That is where we build our own iFrame.[1]

Since we will need to use a *Content Editor* to hold our iFrame text file, we need to add a classic/wiki page (refer back to Figure 93 if needed).

```
<div id="boardParent">
    <iframe id="boardFrame" src="https://plattecanyon.
sharepoint.com/samples/Lists/EventsCalendar/ColorCalendar.aspx"
scrolling="no"></iframe>
</div>
```

Listing 19 shows the styles and HTML that we need.

---

[1]SharePoint uses an iFrame for the Embed/Page Viewer functionality, but we can't control it sufficiently.

Listing 19. Text file containing styles and HTML for displaying a portion of a SharePoint page

```
<style>
    #boardParent {
        overflow: hidden;
        width: 1600px;
        height: 800px;
        position: relative;
    }

    #boardFrame {
        top: -230px;
        left: -200px;
        width: 1600px;
        height: 1000px;
        position: absolute;
        overflow: hidden;
    }
</style>

<div id="boardParent">
    <iframe id="boardFrame" src="https://plattecanyon.
    sharepoint.com/samples/Lists/EventsCalendar/ColorCalendar.
    aspx" scrolling="no"></iframe>
</div>
```

The gist of the solution is that we have an outer *div* tag with an id of *boardParent*. We make its position *relative* so it goes right in line with the rest of the HTML on the page. We make it the size we want for our calendar. We have its *overflow* set to *hidden* so that it won't have any scrollbars. We put our *iFrame* control (id of *boardFrame*) inside this div. We again make it tall and wide. The key is that we position its *top* and *left* with negative numbers. We edit these to that just the portion of the page we want to display is visible. It is kind of like having a piece of paper with a square cutout. We move another paper behind the first one and move that paper so that the portion we want shows through the square.

The browser's *Developer Tools* are a great way to get the *top* and *left* numbers right. Figure 113 shows the initial result.

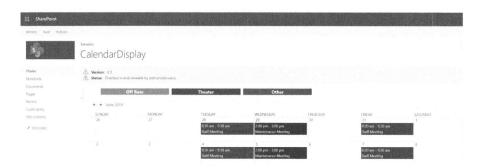

Figure 113. *Initial result of using iFrame to show color calendar before adjusting with Developer Tools*

Notice how the top is cut off while too much of the left is displayed (you can see a little of the month selector). We bring up the *Developer Tools* (F12 in most browsers) and select the *boardFrame* element. We then edit the *top* and *left* values until the calendar is displayed perfectly. This is shown in Figure 114.

Figure 114. *Using Developer Tools to set the top and left of the iFrame*

You will then need to go back and change the text file with the new values since the changes are not written back to the site.

Figure 115 shows the final result.

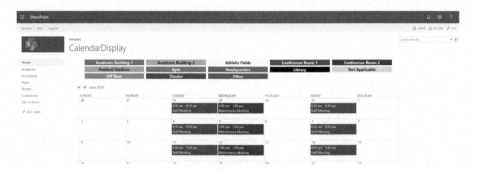

Figure 115. *Final result displaying legend and color calendar on a different SharePoint site*

CHAPTER 19

Creating a Routing System Using InfoPath and Designer Workflows

Microsoft has announced that InfoPath 2013 will be the last version of the product, but it is still supported in Office 365 and looks to be available in the upcoming SharePoint 2019.[1] While it is an older technology, the combination of InfoPath forms and SharePoint Designer workflows is still a powerful combination. This example comes for a request for a way for the cadet squadrons at the Air Force Academy to route approvals through

---

[1]See "What's coming with SharePoint Server 2019 on-premises" at www.techtask.com/whats-coming-sharepoint-server-2019-premises.

© Jeffrey M. Rhodes 2019
J. M. Rhodes, *Creating Business Applications with Office 365*,
https://doi.org/10.1007/978-1-4842-5331-1_19

the appropriate chain of command.[2] Before we created this solution, documents and approvals were emailed from person to person, with no good way to check the status to see where it might be stuck.

Figure 116. *Error message from InfoPath if InfoPath Services are disabled*

By default, InfoPath is not enabled in Office 365. Figure 116 shows the error that you get from InfoPath if InfoPath Services are not enabled. To enable InfoPath, go to the *SharePoint admin center*, select the *infopath* section, and check the *Allow users to browser-enable form templates* and *Render form templates that are browser-enabled by users*. This is shown in Figure 117.

Figure 117. *Enabling InfoPath in the SharePoint admin center*

---

[2]Squadrons are broken into flights and elements. So a cadet who needs approval to travel to a family wedding, for example, might select the *B2* approval, which goes to the B2 element leader, the B flight commander, the cadet squadron commander, and then the air officer commanding.

I prefer to start with a blank form in InfoPath and then create groups (for organization) and fields as shown on the right side of Figure 118. We then drag the fields into the table rows to create the actual controls.

Figure 118. *Creating groups, fields, and controls in Microsoft InfoPath*

My design goal is for the end user to never have to change the InfoPath form. So we put any of the choices or other items that might change into a separate SharePoint list. In our case, the main things that will change are the "approval chains" that show the people that need to approve the current request. We put this in a custom list that we name *Approvers*. We allow up to eight approval levels.[3] Each approver is a *Person* column. This allows us to email the users as well as limit the ability to approve the request on *only* that user.[4]

---

[3]This was a reasonable upper limit in our usage, but you could pick a higher or lower number.

[4]We have found in practice that the squadrons prefer to leave the form open and NOT have the approval locked down for only the named user. This is because cadets might be travelling on an away trip for a sports team or club. Rather than holding up the process, the deputy or a designee will approve instead and put a note in *Approver's Notes* to that effect.

Figure 119 shows adding a new list item,[5] creating a *Data Connection* in InfoPath that points to this list,[6] and then choosing this data connection as the *Data source* for the drop-down list. Notice how to choose the *ID* for the Value and the *Title* for the Display name. This will be important when we create the rules to load the selected approvers from the SharePoint list. When we use the form, the items in the list serve as the possible values.

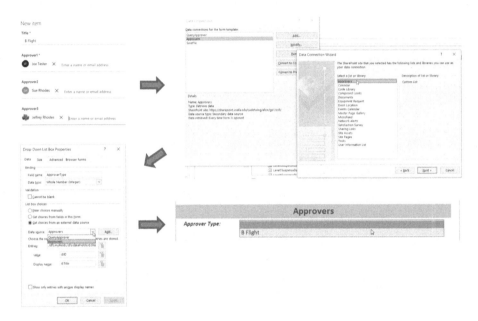

Figure 119.   *Custom Approvers SharePoint list used as the data source for a drop-down list in InfoPath*

Our next step is to configure the approvers. As shown in Figure 120, we put each approver in its own section with a column and associated field

---

[5]Note that only the first approver is required. The workflow logic will figure out how to know when the final approver (2–8) has been reached.

[6]We sort by *Title* and check the box to *Automatically retrieve data when the form is opened* so that drop-down list is ready to go right when the user opens the form.

for *Level, Approver, Suspense, Email,* and *Approved.*[7] The entire section (*Level1ApproverGroup* in the screen capture) has a formatting rule where it is hidden if our *Level1ApproverName* variable is blank.

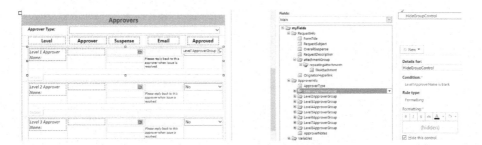

Figure 120. *Organizing the Approver fields into a section that is hidden unless there is an approver for that level*

Since *Level1ApproverName* and the other level variables will all start blank, the approvers are initially hidden. We wait until the user selects an approval chain to show the associated sections and populate their values. Figure 121 shows some of these rules.

Figure 121. *Approver Type rules executed when the user selects an approver chain*

---

[7]The controls with a dotted line around them are *calculated* controls. I use those so that the user is not tempted to type in them. Instead, they are loaded programmatically as we will see shortly.

We have the *DisableIfNotFormCreator* formatting rule to disable the control unless the user is the one who created the form. This helps avoid confusion if someone tried to change the routing in the middle of the process. As shown in Figure 122 to the right, we only execute the rule if the *formCreatorAccountId* variable is either blank or if it doesn't match the current user (which we get using the built-in *userName()* function[8]).

Figure 122. *Formatting rule to disable the control unless the current user is the one who created the form*

Our next task is to look up the approvers in the selected chain. We create a new Data Connection that is similar to the one in Figure 119. We call it *QueryApprovers* to distinguish its purpose. We choose to read all the columns (*Level1–Level8*) so that we can read the names and email addresses of each approver. We don't check the *Automatically retrieve data when the form is opened* box in this case, since we want to wait to execute the data connection until the user selects an *Approver Type*. Figure 123 shows the first rule, *SetApproverId*. This is an *Action* rule where we set a field's value. Very importantly, the field in question is the *ID* in the

---

[8]The *userName()* function is very handy. As we will see later, I commonly have a custom SharePoint list with the authorized users for a particular section of the form listed in the *Person* column. One thing to watch is that you will need to change the column to display the *Account* rather than the default *Name (with presence)* if you will be comparing their values to the *userName()* function.

queryFields part of the *QueryApprovers* data connection. We set its value to be the *Approver Type* drop-down list. Recall in Figure 119 that we set the control's *Value* to be the *ID* and its *Display name* to be the *title*. If we sent into SharePoint and displayed the *ID* column for the *Approvers* list, we could see the actual numerical value that we will use. For those of you familiar with Standard Query Language (SQL), this is the *WHERE* clause. Let's say the *ID* for the approval chain we select is 5, the associated query looks like this (if we expressed it in SQL):

```
Select * from Approvers WHERE ID = 5
```

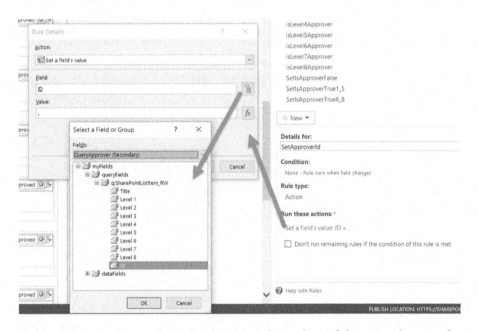

Figure 123. *SetApproverId rule to set the value of the ID column of the queryFields of the QueryApprover data connection*

We have a couple of rules to update the *FormCreatorAccountId* variable and update the hyperlink control to reflect the creator's email address. Both of these take advantage of the *userName()* function.[9]

Next, we have a simple *Action* rule, *QueryApproversData,* to actually run the *QueryApprovers* data connection. We now have our hands on the row of data from the *Approvers* list. We then read the data we want. We have two rules per approver – one to read the name and one to read the account (which we will use in the workflow later to email the approver). Figure 124 shows the first one, *UpdateLevel1ApproverName.* Notice how we read the *dataFields* in this case. Since our SharePoint list column was of type *Person,* we can expand the *Level1* result into *DisplayName* (used here), *AccountId* (used in the subsequent rule), and *AccountType* (not used in our case). We store the result in our *Level1ApproverName* field. This value then displays automatically in the *Approver* column as shown back in Figure 121. The whole Level 1 section will be shown since the formatting rule (Figure 120) kicks in.

---

[9]Getting the proper email address out of the user name requires the use of some functions to strip out the unneeded parts. Here is how it looks for an Office 365 account: `concat("mailTo:", substring-after(username(), "i:0#. f|membership|"), "?subject=", RequestSubject)`. This allows the user to easily launch their email client to send an email the form creator with questions or instructions.

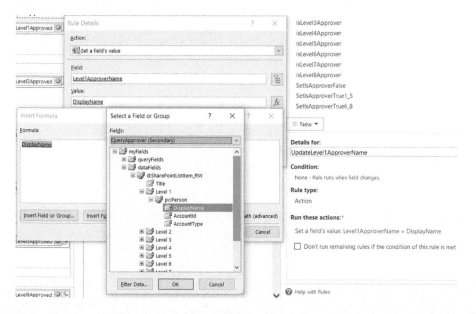

Figure 124. *UpdateLevel1ApproverName rule to read the results of the QueryApprovers data connection*

We use the same technique to update the *Level1ApproverAccountId,* which we will use later to email the approver. We do the same for levels 2–8. Finally, we update variables such as *isLevel1Approver*. This accounts for the situation where the current user is also an approver level. We call this same rule, shown in Figure 126, on the *Form Load* so that approval controls can be disabled unless the user opening the form *is* the approver. This *DisableIfNotApprover* rule is shown in Figure 125 to the right.

Figure 125. *Disabling the approval drop-down box if the user is not the approver*

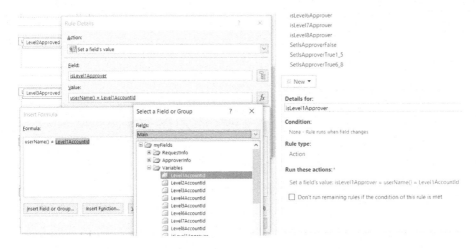

Figure 126. *isLevel1Approver rule to set the appropriate variable based on whether the current user is the approver*

Our last piece of functionality is the *Archive* box as shown in Figure 127. This allows us to move the form to an archive library once the event or other action has occurred. This has the side benefit of removing the form from the associated calendar view that we will show later in this chapter.

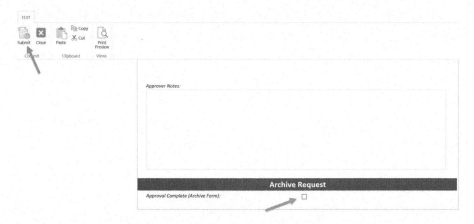

Figure 127. *Archive functionality as well as having a Submit button*

Also shown in Figure 127 is the replacing of the *Save* with the
Submit button. This allows us to store the form in the SharePoint form
library rather than prompting the user to save it locally. The first step in
accomplishing this is to go to *Form Options* ➤ *Web Browser* as shown in
Figure 128. We check the *Submit* box and uncheck the *Save* and *Save As*
boxes as shown in Figure 128.

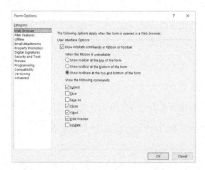

Figure 128. *Showing the Submit button and hiding Save/Save As*

The second step is to choose to save the form *To SharePoint Library*. This creates a data connection as shown in Figure 129. Of key importance is to configure a file name that is unique while not changing when the form is saved over time.[10] In this case we use the *FormTitle* field together with the email of the creator of the form. Notice the use of the *concat()* function to combine the different elements as well as the *substring-after* function to pull out the *i0#.f|membership* part of the account id.

Figure 129. *Saving to a form library with unique file name*

We are now ready to publish. Go to the *File* tab ➤ *Publish* ➤ *SharePoint Server*. If you get the error message shown in Figure 116, then make the administrator changes shown in Figure 117. You will want to choose to publish to a *Form Library*. Check the box to *Enable this form to be filled out by using a browser*. I like to let InfoPath create the form library within the

---

[10]I will often use a date time stamp as part of the title. But if you do this, don't use the *now()* or *today()* functions as part of the form title, as that will make your title change, giving you multiple copies of the same form. Instead, use these functions to set the default value of a field and use that field value in the title. Then the title won't change unless the user manually changes the date (if it is on the form and not hidden).

SharePoint site. We then can add fields from our form to make available in SharePoint. Anything that we either want to display in a SharePoint view or that we want to use in our workflow needs to be added. That's why Figure 130 includes fields like *Level1AccountId*. We need that in order to email the level 1 approver in our workflow.

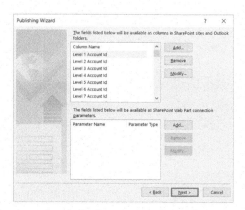

Figure 130. *Adding columns to display in SharePoint and/or use in a workflow*

If your SharePoint form library does not open your form in the browser, then you need to go to *List Settings* and change the *List experience* to *Classic experience* as shown in Figure 131.

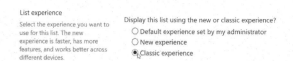

Figure 131. *Setting the List experience in order to display InfoPath forms in the browser*

At this point, the form is operational in that a user can add the information, add attachments, select an approver chain, and save the form.

To implement the rest of the desired functionality, we need to use SharePoint Designer to create a workflow. We select the *Routing* library and then click the *New* button in the *Workflows* section as shown in Figure 132. We name it and take the default *SharePoint 2013 Workflow*.

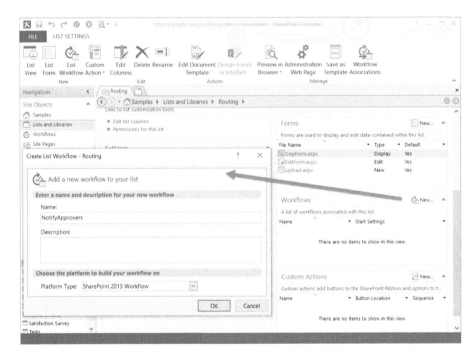

Figure 132. *Creating a workflow in SharePoint Designer*

In order to create the workflow, it is important to understand that the workflow will be run whenever the item (form in this case) is added and/or modified.[11] Of key concern is managing state. For example, we need to consider that the creator of the form may go in and add another attachment or edit text along the way. We don't want to fire off additional emails to

---

[11] I typically use one workflow and run it both when the item is added and when it is modified. This means that you need to take into account both cases when creating your logic.

the current approver in that case. So we need to keep track of where we are. I do this by adding columns of the library itself. For example, the form has the *Level1Approved* field that gets set to true when that approver approves the request. I add a matching column to the library named *Original_Level1Approved* that defaults to false (and is not added to the default view). As we will see later, the workflow has logic to send an email to the Level 2 approver when the *Level1Approved* field is true and *Original_ Level1Approved* column is false. It then sets *Original_Level1Approved* to true. So if the creator goes in and saves the form after that, the workflow won't resend the email. Figure 133 shows all the custom columns.

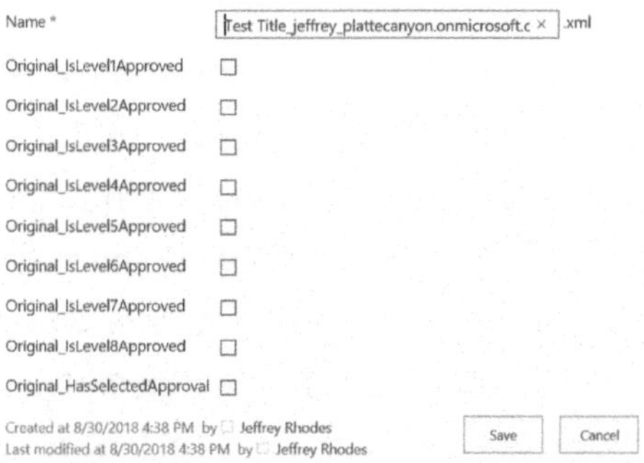

Figure 133. Custom library columns to store the state of the notifications

Workflows are divided into *Stages*. They are basically procedural programs where the stage completes and then the *Transition to stage* block moves execution to either another stage or the *End of Workflow*.

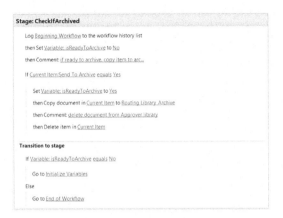

Figure 134. CheckIfArchived workflow stage

Figure 134 shows the initial *CheckIfArchived* stage. Notice the use of the *Log* action, which is helpful for debugging the workflow. It gives messages in the workflow history, which you can access within SharePoint. We then initialize the *isReadyToArchive* variable to *No*.[12] The workflow has a whole *Initialize Variables* stage that comes next, but since we are using this variable right away, we can't wait. Next is a comment that explains our logic. We then have an *if* condition. The *Current Item:Send To Archive* refers to the *Approval Complete* box shown back in Figure 127. As long as we added this column to the publishing to SharePoint (Figure 130), we can read its value. If the box is checked, we set our *isReadyToArchive* variable to *Yes*, copy the form (document) to our archive library, and then delete it in the current library. We use the variable in order to decide whether we transition to the *Initialize Variables* stage (which we will not discuss as it just sets all the variables to a know value) or if we go to the *End of Workflow*. We define all the local variables in the *Workflow Local Variables* screen as shown in Figure 135.

---

[12]InfoPath uses *Boolean* fields where the values can be *true* or *false*. SharePoint itself and SharePoint Designer goes with *Yes/No* where the values can be *Yes* or *No*. These are interchangeable.

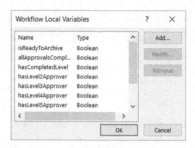

Figure 135. *Local variables within the workflow*

Figure 136. *Notify Level 1 workflow stage*

Figure 136 shows the initial logic of the *Notify Level 1* stage. After a comment to help your successors figure out what is going on, it looks to see if level 1 has been approved already. If so, it uses the *Original_ IsLevel1Approved* column of the library (as discussed previously) to determine if an email to the level 2 approver has already been sent. If so, we set the *hasCompletedLevel* variable to *No*. If not, we set that variable to *Yes* and set *OriginalIsLevel1Approved* to *Yes* (so we don't resend this email). We then check one of the variables that we initialized earlier, *hasLevel2Approver*. If that is *No*, we only had one approver and can set *allApprovalsCompleted* to *Yes*.[13] If we have a level 2 approver, we log a debugging message, create a comment, and then send the email.

Figure 137 shows the editing windows for configuring the *Send an Email* action. We use the *Level 2 Account Id* for the "To" email and the *Form Creator Account Id* for the "CC" email.[14] We use items from the form for the subject, the name of the approver (this is why we loaded the various approver names in the rules back in Figure 124), and the description. Most helpful for the user is a direct link to the form as in the *Click here* hyperlink. The easiest way to build this link is to open an existing form and copy the URL out of the browser. Here is an example:

```
https://plattecanyon.sharepoint.com /samples/_layouts/15/
FormServer.aspx? XmlLocation=/samples/ Routing/
Test%20Title_jeffrey_plattecanyon. onmicrosoft.com.
xml&ClientInstalled=false& DefaultItemOpen=1&Source= https%3A%2
F%2Fplattecanyon%2Esharepoint %2Ecom%2Fsamples%2FRouting%2FForm
s %2FAllItems%2Easpx
```

---

[13]We use the *Level2AccountId* and similar fields from the InfoPath form (see Figure 130) for this purpose. If *Level2AccountId* is blank, then we set *hasLevel2Approver* to *No*.

[14]Notice how both InfoPath and Designer like to put in spaces to make fields and variables more readable. That's why the "To" email shows *Level 2 Account Id*.

We paste that into the "String Builder" dialog and then replace the parts that we can build dynamically:

```
[%Workflow Context:Current Site URL%]/_layouts/15/
FormServer.aspx? XmlLocation=[%Current
Item:Encoded Absolute URL%]&ClientInstalled=false
&DefaultItemOpen=1&Source=[%Workflow Context:Current Site
URL%]%2FRouting %2FForms%2FAllItems%2Easpx
```

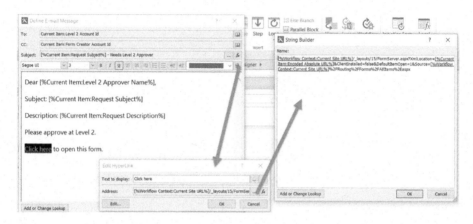

Figure 137. *Configuring the approver email with a hyperlink to the form*

Moving to the *Else* condition, we are in situation where level 1 has NOT been approved yet. In that case, we check the *Original_HasSelectedApproval* column to see if this was the first time the form has been saved after selecting an approval chain. If so, we send the Level 1 Approver email using the same type of email as Figure 137.[15] Finally, we use our *hasCompletedLevel* variable to determine whether we go onto level 2 or jump to our *Notify Original Requestor* stage, which checks the *allApprovalsComplete* variable and, if so, emails the user who created the form.

---

[15]Note that you can copy and paste these actions.

CHAPTER 20

Using SharePoint REST Services to Control Email Notifications

Many of the InfoPath applications that I write involve notification emails and workflows as in the previous chapter. In most cases, however, we want to notify an entire office or workgroup rather than a specific individual. A useful technique is to have each office in a custom SharePoint list. Figure 138 shows the layout of the *Office Members* list. Anyone in this list will have permissions for their office's section of the form. Notice that the *Member Name* column is of type *Person or Group*. We display its *Account* field so that when we reference it from InfoPath, it will match up with its *userName()* function. Later, we will use SharePoint's REpresentational State Transfer (REST) service[1] to read this same list in order to send notification emails to only those members that have a

---

[1]See `https://docs.microsoft.com/en-us/sharepoint/dev/sp-add-ins/working-with-lists-and-list-items-with-rest`.

© Jeffrey M. Rhodes 2019
J. M. Rhodes, *Creating Business Applications with Office 365*,
https://doi.org/10.1007/978-1-4842-5331-1_20

SendNotificationEmails column set to true.[2] While we are at it, we give each user the option for giving one or more *AlternativeEmailAddress* rather than using the one associated with their SharePoint account.

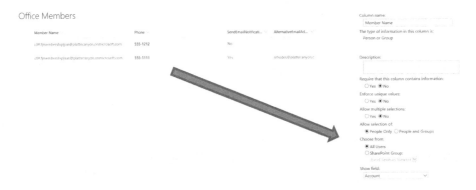

Figure 138. *Office Members list displaying the Account for the Member Name column*

Figure 139 shows our example form. Our workflow will look at the *Submission Complete* box and, when checked, will send an email to everyone in the *Office Members* list (Figure 138) with *SendEmailNotifications* set to yes. Anyone in this list (whether or not they receive an email) can open the form and select his or her name from the *Approved By* list.

---

[2]This gives an easy way for the office to control notifications based on whether someone is in the office. Note that avoiding spaces in the column names is easier since each space needs an encoded _x200_ when using it with REST. Keep them relatively short as well to avoid issues when the names are being truncated.

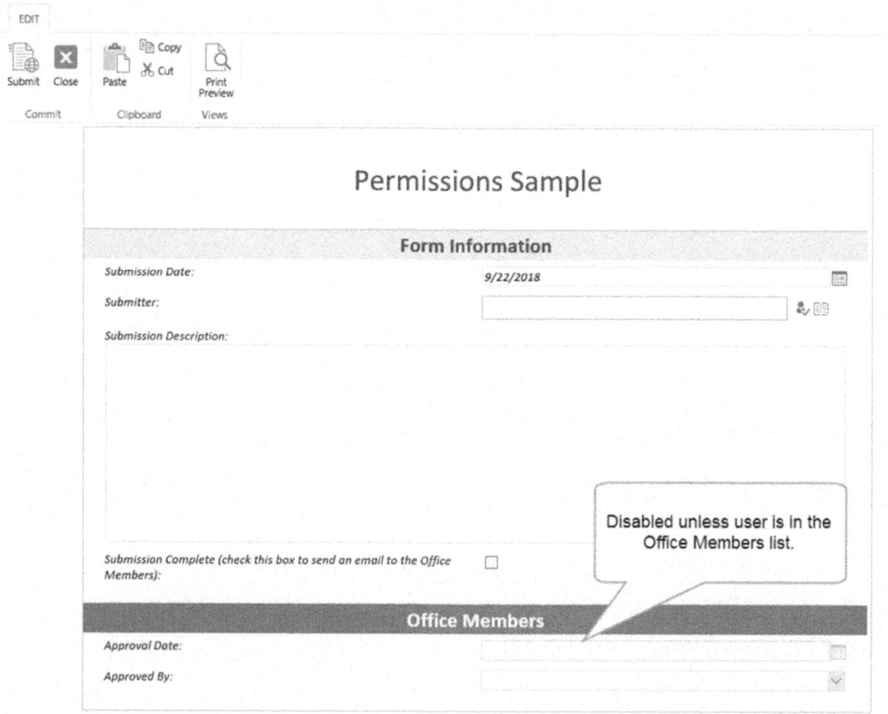

Figure 139. *Example InfoPath form showing the Office Members section disabled for a user not in the corresponding SharePoint list*

You might notice that Figure 139 displays a default date. As shown in Figure 140, we accomplish that by displaying the properties of the *Date Picker* control, clicking the *function* button next to the Default Value, and then inserting the *today()* function. Since this is a default value, the user is welcome to change it. Opening the form on a later date will not cause the form to insert that day's date. If our field value had been a *Date and Time*, then we would have used *now()* instead.

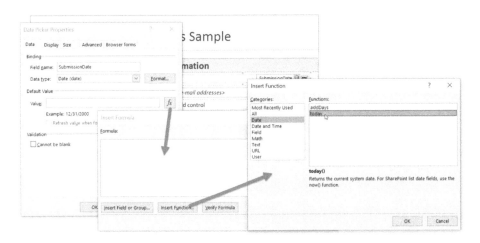

Figure 140. *Giving the form a default date using the today() function*

Our next task is to load the *Approved By* drop-down list with the *Office Members* (Figure 138). We do this by creating a *Data Connection* in InfoPath to read data from that list and then setting this connection as the *Data source* of the list box.

Similar to the logic in the previous chapter, we create an *isOfficeMember* variable and use another data connection, *QueryOfficeMembers*, to set this on the form load. As shown in Figure 141, we set the *Member Name* query field variable. We then set its value to be the current user (Figure 142), taking advantage of InfoPath's *userName()* function. As we discussed in reference to Figure 138, it is important that the display of this column in SharePoint be *Account* so that it is in the same format as *userName()*. Similar to how we approached the previous chapter, we then set *isOfficeMember* based on whether the *count* of the return value of the query is greater than zero and then use that with formatting rules to disable the *Approval Date* and *Approved By* controls if *isOfficeMember* is false.

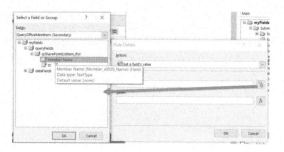

Figure 141. *Setting the Member Name query field value in the QueryOfficeMembers data connection*

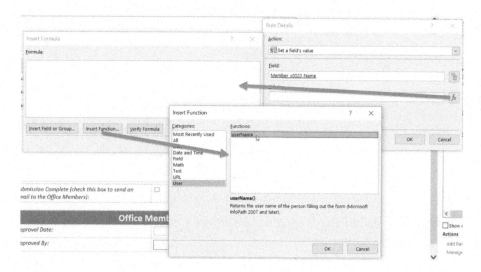

Figure 142. *Setting the Member Name query field to be the current user*

Moving to workflow side of things, the main technical challenge is using the *Office Members* list (Figure 138) to determine who gets emails. For that, we need SharePoint's REST services. Although we will eventually read the results in *JavaScript Object Notation (JSON)* format, it is easiest to use the browser to view the results in XML format. Figure 143 shows how to turn off *feed reading view* in Internet Explorer to get a formatted display.[3] We start by getting all the items in the *Office Members* list using a URL in this format:

```
<site URL>/_api/web/lists/GetByTitle( '<list name>')/items
```

Figure 143. *Turning off Internet Explorer's feed reading view to see SharePoint REST results*

For our sample, this takes this format:

```
https://plattecanyon.sharepoint.com/ samples/_api/web/lists/
GetByTitle('Office%20Members')/items
```

Figure 144 shows the return value for one of the items in the list. Note that the *Member Name* comes through as a number (32) rather than giving direct access to the display name or account of the user.

---

[3]Chrome will display the XML as well but not in a formatted state. In that case, you can paste the results into an XML editor such as *Visual Studio.*

Because of that, we will only need the *Id* of the item (2 in this case). That will then allow us to get user information as well as read columns like *AlternativeEmailAddress*. We also want to limit our responses to only those where *SendEmailNotifications* are true.

```
- <content type="application/xml">
  - <m:properties>
      <d:FileSystemObjectType m:type="Edm.Int32">0</d:FileSystemObjectType>
      <d:Id m:type="Edm.Int32">2</d:Id>
      <d:ServerRedirectedEmbedUri m:null="true" />
      <d:ServerRedirectedEmbedUrl />
      <d:ContentTypeId>0x01008C0AA976EAE42F46AE90AF0C81B92082</d:ContentTypeId>
      <d:Title>555-1111</d:Title>
      <d:ComplianceAssetId m:null="true" />
      <d:Member_x0020_NameId m:type="Edm.Int32">32</d:Member_x0020_NameId>
      <d:Member_x0020_NameStringId>32</d:Member_x0020_NameStringId>
      <d:SendEmailNotifications m:type="Edm.Boolean">true</d:SendEmailNotifications>
      <d:AlternativeEmailAddress>srhodes@plattecanyon.com</d:AlternativeEmailAddress>
      <d:ID m:type="Edm.Int32">2</d:ID>
      <d:Modified m:type="Edm.DateTime">2018-09-23T11:18:09Z</d:Modified>
      <d:Created m:type="Edm.DateTime">2018-09-22T22:17:24Z</d:Created>
      <d:AuthorId m:type="Edm.Int32">10</d:AuthorId>
      <d:EditorId m:type="Edm.Int32">10</d:EditorId>
      <d:OData__UIVersionString>1.0</d:OData__UIVersionString>
      <d:Attachments m:type="Edm.Boolean">false</d:Attachments>
      <d:GUID m:type="Edm.Guid">d22adbd4-8f2e-4beb-a241-0b7f8e734065</d:GUID>
  </m:properties>
</content>
```

Figure 144. *XML return value from the GetListItems() REST method*

We use this URL to limit the responses to the *Id* column and those with email notifications.

```
https://plattecanyon.sharepoint.com/samples/_api/web/lists/
GetByTitle('Office%20Members')/items?$select=ID&$filter=SendEma
ilNotifications eq 1
```

Notice how we use the numeric *1* to represent true. The resulting XML is shown in Figure 145.

Figure 145. *XML return value after using the select and filter properties*

Our next step is to create the workflow(s) using SharePoint Designer. I prefer to use a *SharePoint 2010* workflow to send the actual emails since they are able to send emails to any address.[4] Figure 146 shows the creation of this workflow.

Figure 146. *Creating the EmailUser SharePoint 2010 workflow.*

---

[4]This is important for us at the Air Force Academy because some users have both an "EDU" and "MIL" address. A SharePoint 2013 will only email to the primary account associated with SharePoint, but the 2010 can go to either one (as well organizational email addresses).

Since we will be calling this workflow from our main (SharePoint 2013) workflow, we pass information to this workflow with *Initiation Form Parameters* as shown in Figure 147. We include the various pieces of the email (address, copy address, etc.) as well as the link to the form. Figure 148 shows the *Email* action, the use of the various parameters, and building the hyperlink to the form.

Figure 147. *Initiation Parameters for the Email User workflow*

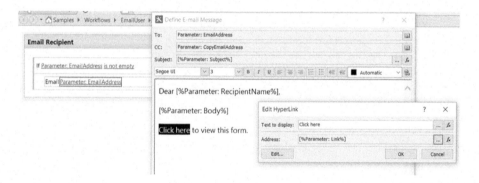

Figure 148. *Configuring the EmailUser workflow in SharePoint Designer*

CHAPTER 21

Creating a Class Sign-Up Solution in SharePoint: InfoPath

I first created this solution for a classroom-based SharePoint training event that we would put on every month. This fairly rapidly expanded to Continuous Process Improvement (CPI) training, numerous personal improvement classes in our community center, to eventually mandatory training for 6,000+ personnel across the Air Force Academy. The gist of the approach is one SharePoint list that holds the classes or other training events (including the capacity of the event) and another list that contains the attendees as well as what event(s) they are signed up for. Views on the list provide a training roster. A user or an owner deleting a registration frees up a spot for someone else. The implementation in this chapter uses InfoPath. See the next chapter for an updated implementation using PowerApps.

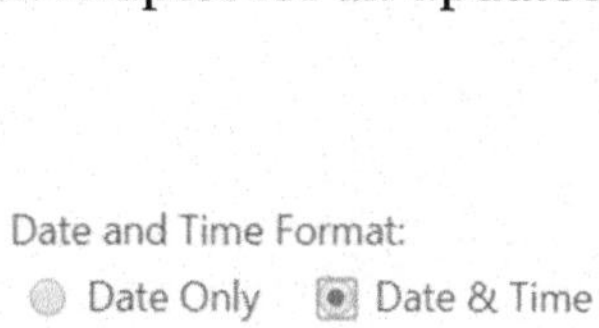

Date and Time Format:
  ◯ Date Only ◉ Date & Time
Display Format:
  ◉ Standard ◯ Friendly

Figure 149. *Setting the date format to Date & Time and Standard*

© Jeffrey M. Rhodes 2019
J. M. Rhodes, *Creating Business Applications with Office 365*,
https://doi.org/10.1007/978-1-4842-5331-1_21

Our first step is to create a custom list that I will name *Classes*. In addition to the default *Title* column, we add *Class Date, Location,* and *Capacity* columns. As shown in Figure 149, we set the format to *Date & Time* and the display to *Standard*.[1] Looking ahead to when we display a list of available classes, we need a column that will show *both* the title and the date/time.[2] So we add a *Calculated* column that we will call *Expanded Title*. Our formula[3] is

```
= [Title] & " (" & TEXT([Class Date], "DD MMM yyyy, HHmm") & ")"
```

This formula takes the title of the class, adds a left parenthesis, formats the *Class Date* in military format with a two-digit day, a three-letter month, a four-digit year, and the hours and minutes in a 24-hour clock.

Classes

ID	Title	Class Date	Location	Capacity	Expanded Title
2	Office 365 Training	8/14/2019 2:00 PM	Room 6J23	10	Office 365 Training (14 Aug 2019, 1400)
1	Office 365 Training	8/6/2019 9:00 AM	Room 6J23	5	Office 365 Training (06 Aug 2019, 0900)
3	Office 365 Training	7/2/2019 10:00 AM	Room 6J23	5	Office 365 Training (02 Jul 2019, 1000)

Figure 150. *The Classes list with some default data, including one event in the past for testing*

---

[1]We need the time so that the user knows what time the class starts. The standard format avoids terms like tomorrow, 2 hours, and the like.

[2]We could put the date and time into the title, but that is messy and subject to error. Plus, we will do logic later to only show classes that are in the future. Trying to get that information out of the title is problematic but easy when we use our *Class Date* column.

[3]On more complicated formulas like this, I recommended copying the formula to the clipboard before clicking the *OK* button. That way, you can paste it in and correct if you get a syntax error and have to start over.

Figure 150 shows the resulting list with some test data, including the bottom class that is in the past as of the time of this writing. This should NOT show up as available in our sign-up form. It will be helpful for making the class roster views to have the *ID* of the class, which is why we added that column to the default view. We also sort by *Class Data* in descending order so that the oldest classes are at the bottom.

Next, we add an *Attendees* custom list. We don't need the default *Title* column, so we will rename it to *Phone* and make it optional. If all our attendees have SharePoint accounts, we can make an *Attendee* column of type Person.[4] Otherwise, we can add individual columns for Name and Organization. Most importantly, we link to the *Classes* list by creating a Lookup column as shown in Figure 151. We don't need any columns other than *ID* since we will handle those in InfoPath.

Figure 151. *Lookup column linking to the ID column of the Classes list*

Our next step is to go to the *Advanced Settings* for the list (Figure 152) and choose *Read all items* and *Create items and edit items that were created by the user*. The first is needed so that we can figure out the capacity from

---

[4]This is a big deal. When we rolled this solution out to all Academy personnel, we added logic where those with account could sign up those without accounts (or even computers). The implementation was similar to what we saw earlier in PowerApps for our Help Ticket solution.

InfoPath. The second prevents chaos where users could delete other users and grab their spots. While we are there, we set the *List experience* to *Classic* so that we get the ability to customize the list with InfoPath.

Figure 152. *Setting proper read/edit permissions as well as the Classic list experience*

The classic list experience allows us to go to the *LIST* tab and select *Customize in InfoPath* as shown in Figure 153. If you do not have this button, refer to Figure 117 on how to enable InfoPath in Office 365.

Figure 153. *Selecting the Customize in InfoPath button on the LIST tab for the Attendees list*

Once you click this button, the form will open in InfoPath. Note that you will be prompted to use Internet Explorer or Edge.

As we see in Figure 154, the initial form leaves quite a bit to be desired. We do get a list of classes, but only their IDs (1, 2, and 3) are shown. We fix that by creating a new data connection that receives data from our *Classes* list. As shown in Figure 155, we add the *Expanded Title* column that we created earlier in the chapter and sort by that as well. We add the *Class Date* so that we can filter out dates that have already passed. We check the *Automatically retrieve data when the form is opened* box so that the data is immediately available. We set that as the data source for our drop-down box, making the *ID* the value and the *Expanded Title* the display. To eliminate past classes, we click the *Entries* button and *Filter Data* and set to only show classes where the *Class Data* is greater than or equal to the built-in *today()* function. The classes now show in a user-friendly manner with any past classes removed.

Figure 154. *Initial Attendees InfoPath form*

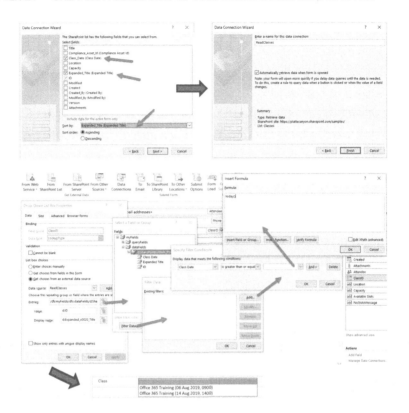

Figure 155. *Creating the ReadClasses data connection and making it the filtered data source for the associated drop-down box*

We add fields to hold *Location, Capacity,* and *Available Slots* information. We change these to *Calculated Value* controls so that they cannot be edited by the user. As shown in Figure 156, we also move the *Phone* control down a row, delete *Attachments*, and rename *ClassID* to *Class.*

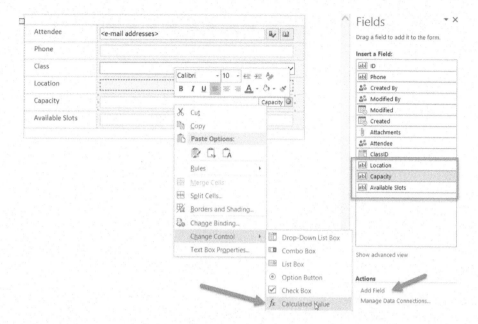

Figure 156. *Adding the Location, Capacity, and Available Slots fields and Calculated Value controls*

The idea is that we wait for the user to select a class. We then use a data connection to read its location and capacity. Note in Figure 157 that we check the *Location* and *Capacity* fields as those are the values we are going to read. We don't bother sorting as we are only going to be selecting a single row of data. We uncheck the *Automatically retrieve data when the form is opened* since we wait to call this programmatically. To do that, we go to the *HOME* tab and click the *Manage Rules* button. We select *Location* as shown at the bottom of Figure 157. We create a new *Action* rule.

Figure 157. *Creating the QueryClasses data connection and adding an Action rule when the user selects a Class*

Our approach is similar to what we saw previously (e.g., Figure 123). For the *SetClassId* rule, we choose *Set a field's value.* For the *Field,* we go to advanced view and select the *QueryClasses* data connection. Since we are reading this data, we set the *ID* queryField. All this is shown in Figure 158. We set the *Value* to be what the user just selected for the class. This is why we set the *ID* to be the *value* of the drop-down list back in Figure 155.

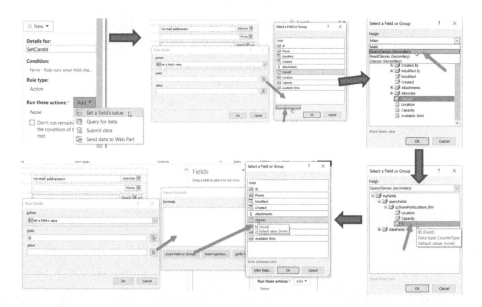

Figure 158. *Setting the ID queryField value to read information for the selected Class*

This sets up the query, but we now need to execute it. For that we create a *Query for data* rule (Figure 159) and tell it to execute our *QueryClasses* data connection.

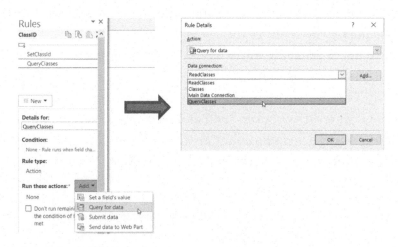

Figure 159. *Configuring a Query for data rule*

Figure 160 shows the process for then reading our data connection and populating the *Location* field. We create a *ReadLocation* action rule. We set the value of the *Location* field and use the dataFields value from our *QueryClasses* data connection. We then do the same for *ReadCapacity*.

Figure 160. *Reading the query results and updating the Location and Capacity fields*

The last screen capture in Figure 160 shows the results. Once we select a *Class,* the rules fire and we populate the *Location* and the *Capacity*. To avoid unwanted decimal places on the *Capacity*, we change the format of its *Calculated Value* control to be a whole number.

The remaining logic revolves around whether slots are available in the selected class. For that, we need to know how many people have already signed up. Luckily, that information is available in our *Attendees* list.[5] As we see in Figure 161, we create another data connection pointing to the *Attendees* class and including our *ClassID* column.[6] As we saw previously, we create a rule to set the queryfield value, but notice in this case we are

---

[5]Recall that the user needs the ability to see all users for this functionality to work. We set this in Figure 152.

[6]You might remember that this is a lookup column from our *Classes* list.

setting the *ClassID* variable to be the *ID* of the *Class* that the user just selected. We then run our *ReadAttendeesForExistingClass* query/data connection.

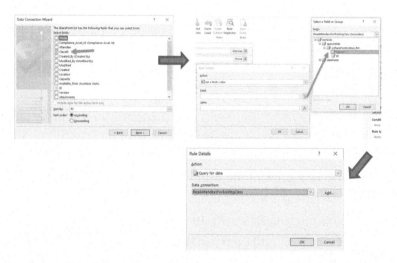

Figure 161. *Data connection and rules to query existing attendees in class*

It is important to understand that this query is in essence a view with two columns (*ID* and *ClassID*) and as many rows where *ClassID* matches our selection. So if ten people have already signed up for our class, this query will return ten rows. This allows us to create the logic for our last rule (Figure 162). We set the value of the *Available Slots* field to be our *Capacity* minus the *count* of our *ID* value. So if our *Capacity* is 15 and our *count(ID)* is 10, the *Available Slots* will be 5.

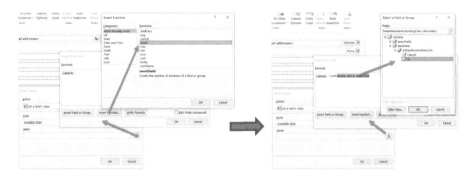

Figure 162. *Using the count function to calculate Available Slots*

So what do we do if there are no more slots available? We'd like to show a message and prevent the user from saving the registration. For the message, we create a *NoSlotsMessage* field and display it in another *Calculated Value* control. As shown in Figure 163, we create a *Formatting* rule to hide this control and then use the *Condition* to hide the field when *Available Slots* is blank (e.g., when the user first opens the form and hasn't selected a class) or when the number of slots is greater than zero (e.g., there are still openings).

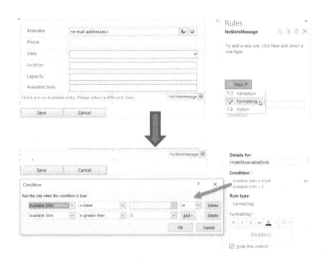

Figure 163. *Creating a Formatting rule to hide message if Available Slots is blank or greater than zero*

To prevent the user from saving a registration for a full class, we first want to disable the *Save* button on the toolbar/ribbon. As we see in Figure 164, we go to the *File* tab ➤ *Submit Options*. We then uncheck the *Show the Submit button in both the Ribbon and the info tab in the InfoPath Filler* box. This results in the *Save* button being disabled.

Figure 164. *Disabling the Submit button for our InfoPath form*

We then add custom Save and Cancel buttons. Figure 165 shows how we use the *Add Rule* button to configure the Cancel button to *Close Form*. We could use this technique for the Save button as well, but instead we use the Button Properties to set its Action to *Submit*. Since our logic is opposite of what we wanted for the *NoSlotsMessage* field, we hide[7] it when *Available Slots* is not blank and *Available Slots* is zero.[8]

---

[7]I would prefer to disable the button rather than hide it. But InfoPath doesn't "gray out" the button when it disables it. So the user is confused on why the button doesn't work.

[8]We use *less than or equal to* zero just in case there is an error condition where the *Available Slots* became negative.

Figure 165. *Configuring our custom Cancel and Save buttons*

Figure 166 shows the form when the user selects a class for which there are no available slots. The *NoSlotsMessage* field shows and the Save button is hidden. Since the *Save* button at the top of the screen is disabled, the user can only cancel the registration or select a different class.

Figure 166. *Registration form with no available slots for the selected class*

Our last task is to create a roster for each class event. Recall back in Figure 150 that we added the *ID* column to our custom view. That helps us build a view for the attendees for each class event. Figure 167 shows an example view. We select the columns we want and sort by our *Attendee* column. Most importantly, we filter our view so that the *ClassID* is for the class in question (1 in our example).

Figure 167. *Custom view for roster of class attendees*

CHAPTER 22

Creating a Class Sign-Up Solution in SharePoint: PowerApps

Let's update the solution from the previous chapter for PowerApps. We reuse our *Classes* list (Figure 150), but one difference that we find between InfoPath and PowerApps is that a drop-down box in InfoPath doesn't default to the first item while PowerApps must have a default. The easiest way to deal with this is to create a new class with a dash as the *Title*.[1] To make sure this default is not filtered out, we make the *Class Date* a long time in the future like 12/31/2099. Since we don't want the date included for our default option, we edit formula for our *Expanded Title* column to be

```
=IF(Title = "-", "-", Title & " (" & TEXT([Class Date],
"DD MMM yyyy, HHmm") & ")")
```

---

[1] Shane Young demonstrates this technique at www.youtube.com/ watch?v=43ekj5MlNJU. He makes a good point that using a dash is easier for debugging than using a space.

© Jeffrey M. Rhodes 2019
J. M. Rhodes, *Creating Business Applications with Office 365*,
https://doi.org/10.1007/978-1-4842-5331-1_22

We use the *IF* function to just put in a dash if the title is a dash. Otherwise, we add the formatted date and time to the class title. Figure 168 shows our *Classes* list with the default entry and new logic.

Classes

Title ∨	Location ∨	Capacity ∨	Class Date ∨	Expanded Title ∨	ID ∨
-			12/31/2099 12:00 AM	-	2
Office 365 Training	6F-100	5	7/2/2019 8:00 AM	Office 365 Training (02 Jul 2019, 0800)	1
Office 365 Training	Heritage Room	10	8/8/2019 10:00 AM	Office 365 Training (08 Aug 2019, 1000)	3
Office 365 Training	6F-100	2	8/22/2019 3:00 PM	Office 365 Training (22 Aug 2019, 1500)	4

Figure 168. *Updated Classes list reflecting a default entry*

For the *Attendees* list, we take a slightly different approach since working with lookup columns in PowerApps is problematic. Instead, we add all the columns that we want: *Class Expanded Title, Class Title, Class Location, Class Date,* and *Class ID.* But we will use PowerApps to link our *Class Expanded Title* to our *Classes* list and then read that list for the title, location, date, and ID.

Figure 169 shows the default *New item* SharePoint form. It is obviously inadequate as there is an entry field (rather than a drop-down list) for *Class Expanded Title* while all the associated columns (title, location, etc.) are editable rather than being loaded automatically. We will fix that by clicking the *Customize with PowerApps* button at the top of the form.

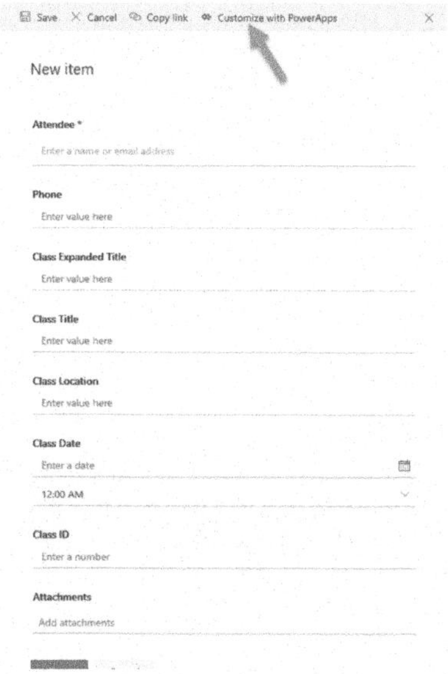

Figure 169. Default SharePoint New item form before customizing with PowerApps

Our first task is to click the *Edit fields* link and remove *Attachments*, which are not needed for our application. Although we don't want *Class Title*, *Class Location*, *Class Data*, or *Class ID* to be editable, don't change them to *View text* here as that ends up preventing PowerApps from writing their data back to SharePoint. We will adjust that later.

We tackle *Class Expanded Title* next. As we saw in previous examples, we unlock the card, delete its DataCard, and add a drop-down list to replace it. We rename it to be *ClassDropDown*. We add a *Data Source* to point to our *Classes* list (you can refer to Figure 98 if needed). In a bit of a quirk with PowerApps, we first set the *Items* property to be our new data source *Classes*. We can then select from the list columns for the *Value* property and choose *Expanded_x0020_Title*. We can save here, publish to SharePoint, and test. We find that the list of classes shows up fine, but it shows classes that have already occurred. To fix that and to sort our items correctly, we change the *Items* to

219

```
SortByColumns(Filter(Classes, 'Class Date' > Now()),
"Expanded_x0020_Title")
```

Working from the inside, we filter the data source so that the *Class Date* is newer than the current date and time (*Now()*). We then sort by our *Expanded Title*. Figure 170 shows the result. Notice how the *Value* is now disabled, which is why we had to set it before updating our *Items*.

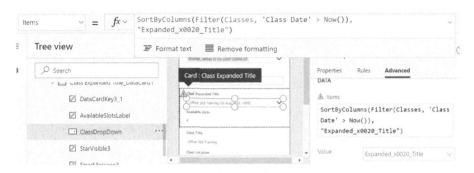

Figure 170. *Setting the Items property of the ClassDropDown control*

This takes care of displaying only upcoming classes, but we still need our control to start with a dash and then have the user select the desired actual class. To do that, we set its *Default* property to

```
If(SharePointForm1.Mode = FormMode.New, "-", ThisItem.'Class
Expanded Title')
```

This uses the dash for a new item but otherwise uses the *Class Expanded Title* from our *Attendees* list.

Our next challenge is to update our associated data (*Class Title, Class Location*, etc.) when the user selects a class. We do that by setting each of their DataCard and their *Default* properties to be the associated column for the selected *Class*. For *Class Title*, it looks like this:

```
If(ClassDropDown.Selected.'Expanded Title' = "-", "",
ClassDropDown.Selected.Title)
```

If the user selects the default dash value, we blank out the *Class Title*. Otherwise, we read the *Title* column value. Since we are setting these values programmatically, we don't want the user to be able to edit them. For that, we set each DataCard's *DisplayMode* property to *DisplayMode. View*.

You may have noticed the *Available Slots* field in Figure 170. We use a similar technique to read the *Capacity* value from our *Classes* list. More concise but analogous to what we did in Figure 162 is using the *Count* and *Filter* functions together to determine how many existing attendees exist for the selected class. The *Text* property of our *AvailableSlotsLabel* is thus:

```
If(ClassDropDown.Selected.'Expanded Title' = "-", "",
ClassDropDown.Selected.Capacity -
Count(Filter(Attendees,'Class ID' = ClassDropDown.Selected.ID).ID))
```

Once the user selects a class, we read its *Capacity* and subtract the number of existing attendees, calculated as the count of the list after we filter the *Class ID* to be the ID of our class.

We are getting close. We just need to show a message if the class is full and prevent the user from saving the item. Since the *Save* button is at the top of the form, we put a *NoSlotsMessage* label there. We set its *Visible* property to

```
!IsBlank(AvailableSlotsLabel) && Value(AvailableSlotsLabel.Text) <= 0
```

Since we want the label to be hidden unless the *Available Slots* is zero (or less than zero to be on the safe side), we show it only if the label is not blank (e.g., a class is selected) AND its numeric text is less than or equal to zero. The *Value* function converts the text to a number. Figure 171 shows this label in action. Notice how the *Available Slots* shows a value of 0.

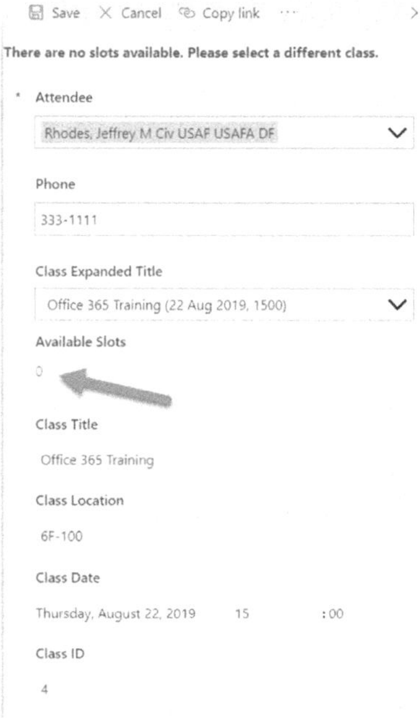

Figure 171. *Form showing "Class Full" message*

Our last task is to prevent the user from saving the item in this situation or when the user has not selected a class. As we see in Figure 172, we select the *SharePointIntegration* item on the left side. That exposed various events like *OnEdit, OnNew,* and *OnSave.* We edit *OnSave* to

```
If(NoSlotsMessage.Visible, false,
If(ClassDropDown.Selected.'Expanded Title' = "-",
false, SubmitForm(SharePointForm1)))
```

We return *false* to prevent saving. We do this if the *NoSlotsMessage* is visible or if the default dash is the selected *Class.* Otherwise we call the *SubmitForm* message.

Figure 172. *Preventing the user from saving the form when a class is full or not selected*

Although it takes some trial and error, overall this is much easier and more straightforward than the InfoPath solution in the previous chapter. Nice job Microsoft!

CHAPTER 23

Adding Google Analytics

While SharePoint is no longer designed for public-facing web sites, it can still be quite useful to track your usage and other data. At the Air Force Academy, our communications management team used to create monthly newsletters that were customized SharePoint pages. Since the built-in usage statistics were fairly primitive (this was SharePoint 2013), I decided to try Google Analytics. Figure 173 shows an example of a *Behavior Overview* report for a particular SharePoint page in Google Analytics.

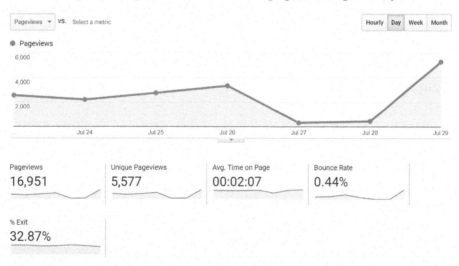

Figure 173. *Example of Google Analytics for a particular SharePoint page*

© Jeffrey M. Rhodes 2019
J. M. Rhodes, *Creating Business Applications with Office 365*,
https://doi.org/10.1007/978-1-4842-5331-1_23

Before jumping into adding Google Analytics to your own page, let's look at how you get built-in statistics in Office 365. You go to the gear button and then *Site usage* or go to *Site Contents* first and then to *Site usage.* Figure 174 shows an example for a lightly used team site.

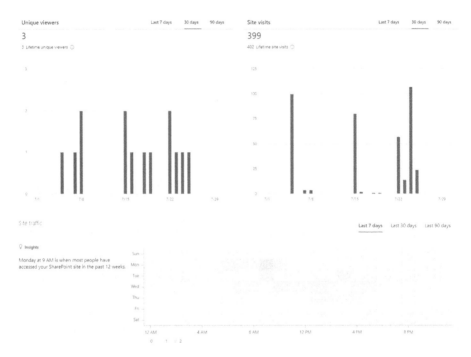

Figure 174. *Built-in site usage in Office 365*

It is much improved over earlier SharePoint versions, but there are still some opportunities for Google Analytics – in particular the ability to see in real time how many users are currently on a particular page and what items on the page they select. Figure 175 shows an example of some of the real-time data.

Figure 175. *Active users with Google Analytics*

We will use the now-familiar technique of putting our desired JavaScript into a text file, uploading it into a document library, and then using a *Content Editor* to embed it into a SharePoint page.[1] You might refer back to Figure 45 for an example.

But first we need to figure out what JavaScript is needed. We create a Google account if needed and go to Google Analytics at `https://analytics.google.com`. As shown in Figure 176, you then create an account, give a name and web site name, choose what information to send to Google, and then get the tracking code (Listing 20).

---

[1]This requires a *Classic* page. See this link for a nice solution for a *Modern* page: `https://sharepoint.handsontek.net/2017/12/21/how-to-add-google-analytics-to-the-modern-sharepoint/`.

Figure 176. *Adding an account and getting a Tracking ID*

Listing 20. Google Analytics tracking code

```
<!-- Global site tag (gtag.js) - Google Analytics -->
  <script async src="https://www.googletagmanager.com/gtag/
  js?id=UA-<tracking code goes here"></script>
  <script>
      window.dataLayer = window.dataLayer || [];
      function gtag() { dataLayer.push(arguments); }
      gtag('js', new Date());

      gtag('config', 'UA-<tracking code goes here');
  </script>
```

We don't have to worry too much about what this code does. Its implementation is in the www.googletagmanager.com/gtag/js location listed previously if you wanted to view in the browser's *Developer Tools*. We add it to a document library, add a *Content Editor* to the page, link to the text file, give a "Do Not Delete" title, and set its *Chrome Type* to None so that the title is only visible when editing the page. All of this is shown in Figure 177.

Figure 177. *Content Editor linking to tracking code*

Figure 178 shows the Google Analytics results after adding the tracking code. Note how it shows the location of the user (myself) as well as the referring site, the number of active users, and other data.

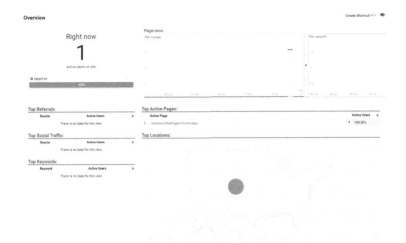

Figure 178. *Google Analytics results after adding tracking code*

Our next step is to track individual events/clicks. For that we use the *Google Tag Manager*: `https://tagmanager.google.com`. In a manner similar to *Analytics,* we create an account (Figure 179) and set *Web* as the target platform.

Figure 179. *Creating a Google Tag Manager account*

Once we create the account, Tag Manager gives us additional HTML and JavaScript (Listing 21), which we add to the text file that we are loading into our SharePoint page with the *Content Editor*.

Listing 21. Google Tag Manager Code

```
<!-- Google Tag Manager -->
    <script>
        (function (w, d, s, l, i) {
            w[l] = w[l] || []; w[l].push({
                'gtm.start':
                new Date().getTime(), event: 'gtm.js'
            }); var f = d.getElementsByTagName(s)[0],
            j = d.createElement(s), dl = l != 'dataLayer' ?
                '&l=' + l : "; j.async = true; j.src =
            'https://www.googletagmanager.com/gtm.js?id=' + i +
                dl; f.parentNode.insertBefore(j, f);
        })(window, document, 'script', 'dataLayer',
        'GTM-<Tag Manager Code Here');</script>
    <!-- End Google Tag Manager -->
    <!-- Google Tag Manager (noscript) -->
    <noscript>
        <iframe src="https://www.googletagmanager.com/
        ns.html?id=GTM-<Tag Manager Coe>"
                height="0" width="0" style="display:none;
                visibility:hidden">
        </iframe>
    </noscript>
    <!-- End Google Tag Manager (noscript) -->
```

Note that you don't have to change this code even after you add tags, triggers, and other Tag Manager elements. In our case, we want some insight into the links and elements on the page that the user interacts with. Figure 180 shows the key steps of the process.

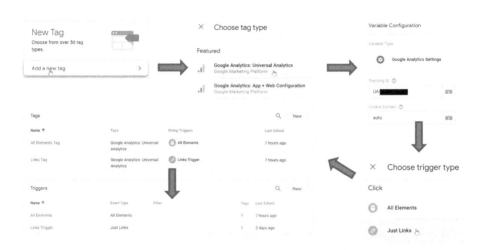

Figure 180. *Configuring tags with triggers to capture each link/click on the page*

We add two tags (*All Elements Tag* and *Links Tab*). We use the *Google Universal Analytics* tag type and configure it with our Analytics *Tracking ID.*[2] For one of our tags, we use the *All Elements* trigger type, while we use *Just Links* for the other one.

Tag Manager has a nice debugging feature. You click the *Preview* button and then open your page in a separate tab in the same browser. There is then a Tag Manager preview window at the bottom of the page as shown in Figure 181. Each click is shown in the *Summary* pane at the left. You can select each one such as the *Click* link shown and then get information about the event such as the URL.

---

[2]We store this in a variable so that we can use it for both of our tags.

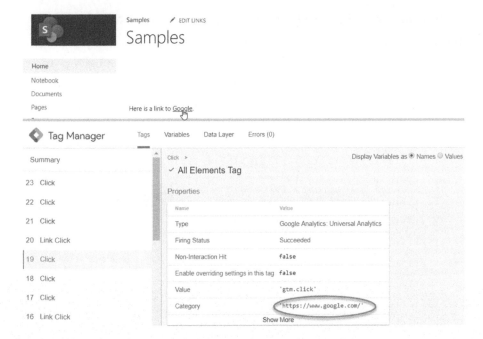

Figure 181. *Debugging in Google Tag Manager*

We can then see the individual events with Google Analytics as shown in Figure 182.

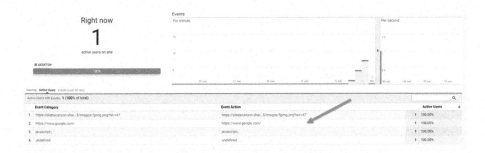

Figure 182. *Seeing Tag Manager events within Google Analytics*

If we have a team site connected to a group,[3] you can add a *Google Analytics* connector to a modern SharePoint page. Figure 183 shows the steps for adding the connector. It prompts you to log into Google, give permissions, select the account and application, and select the frequency. The connector then inserts the most recent statistics into your page.

Figure 183. *Adding a Google Analytics connector to a modern SharePoint page*

---

[3]It is not clear why at least some of the connectors are not available for communications and standard team sites. I suspect that will be opened up at some point.

Index

A

Accordion interface
    accordionDesign.txt,
        style section, 80
    blog posting, 78
    content editor referencing, 78
    document.ready function, 83
    FAQ sections, 77
    logic, 81, 82
    MyPageLoaded function, 83
    section setting, 79
    toggleClass method, 84
    UpdateToggle function, 83
Alert, 30, 32–33
Announcements list, jQuery
    affected network
        EDU, 31
        MIL, 31
    associated class, 33, 34
    calculated column, 30
    choice columns, 29, 30
    developer tools, 35, 36
    EDUNotExpired view, 31
    ms-cellstyle, 38, 39
    ms-vb2 classes, 38, 39
    network alerts, 32–34, 36, 37

title column, 30
    USAFAOperational class, 35
Attendees list, 203
    custom view, 215
    dash value, 220
    data connection, 211
    InfoPath form, 205
    LIST tab, 204
    PowerApps, 218
Available slots
    cancel/save button, 214
    class full, 222
    count function, 212
    registration form, 214
    saving the form, 223

B

BaseRecord parameter, 141
Built-in site usage, 226
built-in today() function, 151, 205
button() method, 28

C

Calculated Value controls, 207,
    210, 212

Printed by Printforce, the Netherlands